Where *the* Light Gets In

Where
the
Light
Gets In

Stories about the
**Transformative Power
of One Action**

JILL TREMLETT LARGE

Pen & Publish
Saint Louis, Missouri

Published by Pen & Publish, LLC, USA

www.PenandPublish.com
info@PenandPublish.com

Saint Louis, Missouri
(314) 827-6567

Paperback ISBN: 978-1-956897-41-8
Hardcover ISBN: 978-1-956897-48-7
e-book ISBN: 978-1-956897-42-5
Library of Congress Control Number: 2024939257

Cover Design: Laura Duffy
Cover Art: Eugenia Ortiz, eugeniaortizart.com
Author Photo: Leslie Koehn

The stories in this book are all true; however, in some instances, names or details may have been altered to protect safety and confidentiality.

Readers should take note that this book contains descriptions of physical, emotional, sexual, and financial abuse. If you are experiencing intimate partner abuse and need help, please contact the National Domestic Violence Hotline at 800-799-7233.

Caring for others more than we do for ourselves
is the most rewarding thing in life.

If enough people help other people, and those people help others, and
on and on, you can have amazing results.

—Doris Eleanor Buffett (February 12, 1928–August 4, 2020)
Founder, Women's Independence Scholarship Program, Inc

I'm so grateful that my story continues to inspire others.

But it's just my story.
We all have stories worth listening to.

We can create empathy that grows into compassion by sharing our stories and creating space for others.

All of us are capable of starting a movement.

—Stephanie Land
Author of *Class* (2023) and *Maid* (2019)
Executive producer of Netflix miniseries *Maid* (2021)
WISP recipient (2011–2013)

If I held a hummingbird

If I held a hummingbird, centered in my palm, it would be beautiful, beautiful

And if I were held, finally unharmed, it would be beautiful, beautiful

If we harmed less and held the harmless, it would be beautiful, beautiful

And if we felt less harmed and more hope-full, it would be beautiful, beautiful

If we were full—up to eyebrows—with fuel and love and open palms—it would be beautiful, beautiful

And if we loved fully, from brows to toes, it would be beautiful, beautiful

If I could breathe wishes into love and hummingbirds into truth, it would be beautiful, beautiful

And if I wished only bare love, for you, for me, it would be beautiful.

—Rebecca Evans
Author of *Safe-Handling* (Summer 2024)
Author of *Tangled by Blood* (2023)
Coeditor of *when there are nine* (2022)
WISP recipient (2012–2016)

Contents

Introduction:
WISP at Twenty-Five

It was in Denver, Colorado, at the National Coalition Against Domestic Violence conference in 1998, that the first-ever Sunshine Peace Award winners were honored. The award was the brainchild of Doris Buffett and was designed to recognize advocates for the challenging work of helping women escape domestic violence.

During dinner, Doris found herself in a conversation with an award winner and a survivor of domestic violence. This is where she learned of a key reason women fail to leave abusive relationships—they are afraid they won't be able to provide for themselves and their children.

As Doris listened, a powerful thought arose. *We can fix that!*

It was the spark that would become the Women's Independence Scholarship Program (WISP).

Now, twenty-five years later, WISP has helped over 2,600 women graduate from an educational program of their choosing. WISP has faced the fear that so many women in abusive situations experience and provided a solution: the funds to pursue an education to attain job security and professional success, and the confidence of knowing that they are capable of taking care of themselves. At the twenty-five-year mark, WISP has awarded over $47 million in scholarships to qualified applicants.

All of this is owed to the vision and optimism of one benefactor: Doris Buffett.

Doris had a long history in philanthropy before WISP, but not as long as one might think. When your last name is Buffett, people assume you were born wealthy and lived a life of privilege. But that wasn't the case. To understand the story, you have to meet the woman.

Doris Eleanor Buffett was born in Omaha, Nebraska, the eldest in a family that included her younger and ultimately financially famous brother, Warren. Doris's mother suffered from depression and possibly other illnesses that affected her parenting. She was emotionally abusive to young Doris and frequently told her daughter that she was unworthy and dumb, undermining Doris's efforts to seek higher education.

This treatment impacted Doris into adulthood. She was married four times, was estranged from her children for many years, survived two bouts of cancer, and battled periods of depression. While she initially owned shares of her brother's company, she was the recipient of poor financial advice and lost most of her money in the 1987 stock market crash. Even as Berkshire Hathaway boomed, Doris was clipping coupons, trying to eke out a living renting out a room in her home.

But none of this dimmed her optimism—the personality trait that earned her the childhood nickname "Little Mary Sunshine." And when Doris did come into money—a $10 million inheritance from her mother—she was inspired to take the funds she'd received and the empathy she'd developed and turn it all into philanthropic efforts.

She started the Sunshine Lady Foundation in 1996. Its early initiatives included sprucing up domestic violence shelters in a way that would reflect the worth and dignity of the women and children staying there and funding the education of grassroots leaders in the domestic violence field. Why domestic violence? Maybe because of her own unhappy family relationships. Or maybe her experience helping to start one of the first safe houses in the country played a role. Whatever the influences were, they led her to create an innovative response to the problem of intimate partner abuse.

That conversation at the Sunshine Peace Awards showed Doris her next step. She had great faith in education as a means of opening doors of opportunity and believed it could be a way to break the cycle of economic abuse by providing access to better and more stable employment. And she was especially empathetic since her own mother had made her educational journey so difficult. Doris started the Women's Independence Scholarship Program in 1999, just one year after that pivotal conversation. In its first year of operation, WISP awarded 124 scholarships with a total of $194,252 granted. Over the next ten years, 3,500 awards were made, totaling over $19 million in financial assistance.

"I am profoundly grateful to have been a small part of the WISP legacy," says Peggy Pasin. She sponsored the very first WISP recipient and went on to facilitate scholarships totaling over $2.7 million during the nineteen years she worked with students at Utah Valley University. "The lives of scholarship recipients changed so dramatically. Education lifted those survivors out of their dependency and empowered them to see themselves as capable, strong, intelligent, and able to accomplish amazing feats."

Each WISP applicant is required to partner with an advocate or case manager at a nonprofit organization in her community that is familiar with the dynamics of intimate partner abuse. WISP calls these partners "sponsors" and relies on them to link scholars with local supports and resources. It's a collaborative effort—and as a sponsor, Peggy valued that connection with WISP staff. "I could call and talk to my contact at WISP and she would always make time for me. It was a feeling of being on a team. I never felt alone." She forged a special connection with Doris as well. "She gave me her phone number and we had many lovely conversations where she shared her excitement about WISP, the women who worked there, and other projects."

WISP changed Peggy's life too. "I didn't think domestic violence was at all prevalent where I lived. Discovering the reality was such an eye-opener and I then dove into learning everything I could about it. I learned richly, and I thrived on that learning."

In 2008, backed by a $30 million endowment from Doris, WISP became its own separate organization. Doris passed away in 2020. But her legacy of fighting for the underdog and engaging in personal, one-to-one "retail" philanthropy lives on. Doris used her personal misfortunes and her financial good fortune to change the world. That was her unique gift.

Now, in 2024, WISP celebrates its milestone of helping thousands of women pursue the educational path of their choosing. Empowering applicants by allowing for any degree program is a cornerstone of WISP—as long as the school and coursework are accredited and there's a clear path to a degree.

Many students choose traditionally female-oriented sectors, like social work, nursing, and education. But WISP has also sent women to school for engineering, computer science, and construction management. WISP funds trades and certificate programs, like welding, electrical apprenticeships, cosmetology, and machining. And then there are choices that come along more rarely—equine science, fisheries technology, piano pedagogy, somatic psychology, sports management, and even shoe design.

While so much thought and planning went into the creation of WISP, twenty-five years of experience has revealed a dramatic, surprising, and unintended impact: It has become a badly needed voice of support for the women who were making their way out of abuse. A hallmark of the emotional abuse that is present in intimate partner violence is the systematic dismantling of the target's self-worth as a means of exerting control and dominance. WISP has always gone beyond simply writing a check and made efforts to encourage and support program participants with gifts, motivational emails, inspirational quotes, and a liberal sprinkling of the signature gold sun and star glitter included in every mailing. These actions have created a sense of community, and these connections are healing—especially so for people who have been intentionally isolated as part of the abuse cycle. It's become clear that this is another crucial part of breaking the cycle of abuse.

Everything WISP does is with the intention of honoring Doris Buffett's wish that each scholarship recipient go on to live a "full and triumphant life." And that's a story to be proud of.

But to really understand the impact of WISP, you need to meet the women. For this project, a group of WISP graduates volunteered to share their own personal stories of what the "gift of WISP" meant to them, and how that gift has rippled out into the lives of their families and their communities. In sharing their stories, they are giving us a gift—demonstrating that each of us individually has the power to change the world simply by sharing the gifts that are uniquely ours.

When a glass or a bowl breaks, we might think that it is ruined. Whether they're just small fractures or it's been smashed into smithereens, it doesn't look the way it used to. We fear it can't function like it could before.

The same can be said of a life that takes a sharp turn to something that's unexpected, unwanted, or even disastrous. Intimate partner violence can break a life apart, leaving fractures both visible and invisible. A life that doesn't go as planned may seem ruined.

Unless there's a way to see it differently.

The Japanese art of kintsugi centers on the idea that there is beauty in the broken. Pottery that has been shattered is mended using gold and silver epoxy. When refired, the former breaks now shine. An object once considered ruined becomes something even more beautiful than its original state. The basic, everyday vessel is elevated to art. It is better for having been broken.

Can it be true, then, that a human life that seems broken could also be mended in the same way? Could it be that there is beauty in the scars?

The stories in this book suggest that the answer to those questions is yes. Each storyteller has mended her wounds with her own unique firing of resilience, grit, grace, determination, love, tears, and faith. They have transformed their pain into a gift that they share with the world around them. And they did it all with intent. On purpose. By choice.

There's a hidden truth to those broken pieces that look so ugly: The cracks are where the light gets in.

You'll experience the truth of that statement as you read the inspiring tales of emergence from domestic abuse, leveraging education to move forward, and giving back to the community that supported their efforts. The hardships that each storyteller encountered are the fuel that feeds their actions today—to make a difference in someone's life, to change systems for the better, to challenge the status quo.

Each of their stories is unique and personal, and somehow each is also universal. You'll hear common themes: the challenge of feeling worthy, the fear of failure, and the inspiration that comes from others showing support. You may hear snippets of yourself in some of the stories, and at the same time, you might be surprised or even shocked at what you see on the page. The true gift of this book is in the sharing of story. Thomas Merton said, "We make ourselves real by telling the truth." When we reveal our truth, we feel less alone. When we find commonality in those stories, others feel less alone too. This is how we are all connected.

When you know the stories of the women in this book, you'll experience that sense of connection, and you will become a part of what Doris created.

Glitter

RECEIVING A SCHOLARSHIP FROM WISP is a cause for celebration, and that's why we include gold star confetti in everything we mail out. It's a little party in every package. This has been our delight since the first WISP award letters were mailed, and in twenty-five years of sending letters and gifts to scholarship awardees, we like to think we've added a bit of sparkle to nearly every post office in the United States.

Not only is it pretty, shiny, and fun—WISP recipients tell us that our star confetti has come to symbolize something greater.

It's a reminder that even the smallest gesture can have a big impact.

> The first time I opened a package from WISP I was astounded by the tiny gold stars that were everywhere. My boys fought over them, we stuck them on our cheeks and foreheads! I thought it was an adorable novelty.
>
> Those stars have shown up in every single package from WISP. They've come to mean so much to me. They remind me to shine bright like a star. To reach for the stars always. And most importantly, that I am the star of my own life. I control the narrative; I decide my fate.
>
> That may seem like a given for some people, but for me, it is a revelation and gives me the strength to never look over my shoulder again. Much. I'm still growing.
>
> I love the stars and I will miss them very much when I graduate.
>
> —Jolene

When I opened the envelope from WISP, I didn't realize that I was spilling beautiful little gold stars everywhere! But my little boy did! My head was all over the place. I knew that I was trying to create a new life for me and mine.

I kept finding those stars everywhere, and every time I would, I was further on my road to recovery and the rest of my life. The WISP scholarship has been a huge support to my family—this would be so much harder without all the support I have—and I still find those gold stars!

—Anonymous

There were five semesters total in my nursing program. I was working three part-time jobs. I was on government assistance for housing and food. I had a 2007 Toyota Camry I named Sallie Mae. However, Sallie Mae's dash melted. It was sticky all year long. I had to make the best of a sticky situation, so I began sticking my fortunes from my fortune cookies, small shells, and dried flowers my kids had picked for me on the dash.

When I received my first WISP package, I sat in my car and cried. I was able to cut back at work to be able to spend time with my kids and study. I had never been more grateful. In that moment, I allowed my intrusive thoughts to win and just started shaking and pouring those golden stars all over my dash. On the mornings that it was hard to get motivated for school, those shining stars always added a little extra glitter to even the gloomiest days.

—Kandace

I love the stars you all mail. I spread them across my office desk. It makes me feel really special and good inside.

—Ariel

I opened the WISP scholarship envelope and found gold star glitter in it. It brought up my magical childhood memories of end-of-the-year holiday celebrations—those days glitter was on the Christmas tree toys. It was on my dresses that Mama decorated for school events and parties. It was on posters that me and my aunt made for school. It was on the postcards that we sent and received. I treat my special memories with care. It was a time when I was taken care of. I was loved. I felt secure.

I have visited my home only three times in the twenty-five years of living in the USA. Life gave me many hard lessons. Constantly overcoming life's difficulties has been exhausting. At times, being without help felt hopeless. To hold to my good memories, I put glitter on my nails, on the oil paintings that I make, and on my room decorations. I add glitter everywhere I can.

I opened the WISP scholarship envelope and found gold star glitter in it. I gathered the stars and put them in a little bag. They came with priceless decorations to my life—scholarship, the possibility of studying, getting an education, and a job. The possibility of creating myself.

Some people add magic to the lives of others and spread goodness. The path is right, the people are caring, and the hope is alive.

—Svetlana

It took me a while to wrap my brain around the concept of scholarships. Why would someone pay for me to succeed? Why would someone just voluntarily give me something that would help me get ahead in life?

I've always valued the concept of charity and helping one another. I've witnessed people doing kindness my whole life. I've always tried being kind and helping other people myself. Years of abuse had led me to believe that I'm different. I don't deserve kindness. Whenever I received kindness, there was a voice in my head telling me that if people would only know how damaged I am, they wouldn't have helped me. The voice in my head was merely an echo of years of abuse.

WISP helped me change that belief, by believing in me.

I'm not ashamed to admit that I saved these glitters that fell out of the envelope. It meant so much to me. It made me feel human. It made me feel that I am part of something bigger and that I'm being supported. I'm worthy to be thought about.

These gold star glitters brought sunshine into my life.

—Anonymous

Ask and Receive

Linda's Story

EVERY DAY AT WORK, Linda holds life in her hands.

A clinical perfusionist for heart bypass surgery at a major hospital, Linda is in the operating room scanning for potential problems with the patient while the surgeons do their meticulous work.

"I operate the heart-lung machine, which temporarily replaces or assists the heart and lungs of our patients." She acknowledges that the job can be very demanding and stressful. It takes an incredible amount of care to attend to even the slightest change before it becomes life-threatening. Because of what she calls "the gift" of WISP, she cares for each of her patients the way she feels like WISP cared for her, recalling the days when she was fresh out of a terribly abusive relationship and in desperate need of help.

"Every day, I think about the scholarship award I received from Mrs. Doris Buffett. I am so grateful for the opportunity she gave me so many years ago. I work hard every day to improve the quality of life of others. I am simply continuing the gift you all gave to me."

Linda, one of the earliest recipients of a WISP scholarship, can reflect on how dramatic her journey has been—from an abusive marriage that felt "like being trapped in a deep, dark hole" to a place of professional responsibility and personal joy.

"WISP was a flashlight and a rope that pulled me out of that dark place. I was so beaten down that I couldn't get out on my own." And today, she recharges by finding joy in everything. "It's everywhere. Even driving my son to school—wonderful! It's our perception that creates our reality," she says.

It was more than two decades ago that Linda, who'd always considered herself a positive, resilient person, felt she'd lost sight of who she was and how she could live a happy life. With the help of a local domestic abuse organization, she was able to leave her marriage. It was then that she realized education would be her road forward.

"School will save me," she recalls thinking. "An education will keep me on the path for what I always wanted." She applied to a college program and was accepted. She then spent six months researching and applying for aid—everything from well-known programs to niche scholarships, such as one offered by the Vlasic Pickle company, aimed at students of Croatian heritage. It was during that search that she became aware of WISP.

"I get emotional—in a good way—when I think about what the scholarship meant. Life-changing is an understatement," she says. "WISP gave me hope. I got my life back. I got myself back. WISP enabled me to be the person I knew I was."

One of the key ways WISP was critical to her success was how it was supportive in what many would consider nontraditional ways for a scholarship program. Part of the core mission of WISP is to provide financial assistance for expenses that would otherwise be barriers to education—like fixing a car, paying for childcare, or helping with housing costs. In Linda's case, WISP helped make sure her basic needs were met, so she could focus on the business of learning.

Linda was enrolled in school and focused on her degree—but still feeling the aftereffects of her abusive marriage. "He made sure we had no money," she recalls. "I would open the refrigerator and there would only be one slice of cheese. I would remind myself it's not always going to be this way. It will get better."

And when unexpected setbacks popped up, WISP was supportive. "Someone hit my car in the parking lot while I was at clinicals," she relates. The repair bill came to $1,300. "It wasn't drivable, and I had zero money." Linda reached out to WISP and a check was overnighted to her. Linda recalls the enclosed instruction: *Get that car fixed and go to school!* WISP knew what she needed to move ahead.

After graduation, Linda worked first with babies in the neonatal intensive care unit. Then she worked in the OR. "I am incredibly positive in the operating room because I know how fragile we all are," she says. "I share my joy with others who are experiencing a dark time in their lives. They had other plans for the day and their lives were interrupted by an urgent medical need, and it's my mission to do everything within my power to make sure that they can get back to the things that are important to them, and so that they have the opportunity to reach their greatest potential." She does this with intention, she says, because that's what WISP did for her so many years ago.

Linda reflects on the way WISP helped her to be in this critical professional role. "I have been with our program for fourteen years, and I have helped many patients over the years. My goal for every patient is to send them home and allow them to live a better quality of life with their loved ones. I love that I am a part of something so wonderful." Linda sees her joy as a currency—one she shares generously, just as Doris was generous with financial and emotional support through WISP.

Linda doesn't regret or begrudge anything that happened in her past. "It's all taken me to where I am now. I'm a happy mom, I've shown my sons an example of resilience, confidence, and grit. Now I encourage them to go to school and achieve their maximum potential in life."

She keeps a memento of her journey on her desk. Back in 1999, WISP recipients received their acceptance letters in the mail, in an envelope that contained the letter and a handful of gold sun and star confetti. For the two years that she was involved in the program, Linda gathered all her confetti and now keeps the suns and stars in a jar on her desk. "I look at them every day and stir them with my finger because it's fun and pretty. They shimmer and radiate light and remind me of the day my life completely changed."

And it's a reminder that the right support at the right time can make all the difference.

Her message: Don't try to go it alone. "I want other women who are where I was to know that it's not always going to be this bad. There are people who want to help them, and that strength comes from asking for help."

She shares her story as proof that transformation is within reach, no matter what. "When you see someone else doing it, you realize it's possible."

It's All Divinely Inspired

Jane's Story

WHEN JANE WAKES UP in the morning, she often thinks about the way her experience with domestic violence has affected her, and her thoughts tend to drift in a positive direction.

"I don't have to worry about him anymore, so I'm just grateful. I wake up every morning in peace and silence. I never thought I'd ever say this; it was one of the best things that ever happened to me—surviving all that."

She thinks of each challenge she's overcome as a blessing in disguise and firmly believes that everything in her life is divinely inspired. And she recognizes that hindsight helps her make sense of what's happened. "It's only when we get through it that we can look back and see all the pieces of the puzzle," she says. "That has helped me to realize no matter what's going on in my life today, and no matter how difficult it looks like, I know deep down in my gut that it's all a part of God's plan for my life and it's going to all work out exactly the way it's supposed to."

Developing her spiritual foundation has been a lifelong quest.

"I didn't grow up in a religious, spiritual home. Went to church with the neighborhood lady. I didn't really know anything but Kool-Aid and cookies when I went there." It was through her engagement in a support group that she was propelled further down the spiritual path. "I went to lots of meetings, but I was miserable." There came a point of surrender. "I got on my knees and I said, *Okay, God, if there's anything to this Jesus stuff, you need to come down here and show me because I'm not getting it.* Two weeks later, I was in a Pentecostal church. And they said, *Does anybody want to be saved?* Well, I knew didn't know any of this stuff, but my arm went up by itself. The next thing they said was, *Anybody here want to be baptized in the Holy Spirit?* I had no clue what they were talking about—but my arm went up again. These women took me in this back room and they started laying their hands on me and praying over me. And one of them told me to start praying out loud in Jesus's name. I had a major white-light experience. I lost my eyesight. I lost my hearing. I couldn't see anything. I was blinded. And when I came out of it, it was like a big gush of wind went through me and I started to cry uncontrollably."

It was her abuser who pointed out that her experience wasn't about that particular church. God chose to show Himself to her because she asked. The experience caused her to think more deeply about herself, her faith, and her place in the world.

Today she is in a place of peace, secure in the knowledge that "if it was not for my ex, I wouldn't be where I'm at right now. I would have never had what I have in my life now. And I don't mean materialistically. I mean the growth that I've experienced with spirituality."

Still, it was a treacherous journey to get there.

"I grew up in alcoholism and said I would never become one," says Jane. But it was not that simple, and Jane battled addiction as a young woman. "I have had a lot of relapses in my life—not chemicals, but mainly co-dependency relationships. I felt like all my life I had this great big hole in my soul and this void. I just felt like if I had somebody that loved me, I would be okay. And I went through what I like to call the Marriage Series. It was just rinse and repeat. My last husband was the icing on the cake. He was the domestic violence piece."

They had a child together, and soon after her son was born, he became ill. She had to give up her career to stay home and take care of him, and that's when she could clearly see the situation worsening.

"I stayed at home for seven years. And of course, that gives an abuser all the control," she says.

But as Jane looks back at that time in her life, she realizes that everything happened according to God's plan. Giving up her job to take care of her son was an opportunity for Jane to become more engaged in her own spiritual journey. "When I was there in that house, I started really seeking on a different level. And it wasn't in a church. It was with a couple of women who I'd met and we would talk and pray." This connection with other women in an informal prayer group was the beginning of her exploration of what she called "radical spirituality." She credits her deep spiritual connection with being able to survive in a marriage that could have turned deadly on more than one occasion.

"I remember one incident, particularly, where my ex-husband, a big man, picked me up by the throat and pulled his fist back to punch me and said, *Where's your effing God at now?* I think he had so many demons and so many problems that he never dealt with. I went through a whole period of trying to change me to keep him from doing it. And then the day came when it wouldn't matter if I said the sky is blue and he said the sky is green. If he said it's green, it was going to be green."

Jane looks back at incidents like this knowing that some women don't survive them, being grateful that she did, and feeling like they were given to her by God to be able to help others.

Over time, her abuser's behavior began to affect her son, and he was removed from school.

"We were mandated to go to therapy. The first meeting had to be just the parents. We meet at the therapist's office, go in, and I sit there and listen to an hour of what's wrong with me from him. This was one of my first moments of clarity in the middle of this abuse. It's like waking up, and I thought, *I am sick and tired of living like this.* My household looked perfect. He made a lot of money. He had custom Harley-Davidsons, four new cars in the driveway, diamonds—I looked the part. But it was like living in hell inside the house with him. And I thought to myself, sitting there, *I'm going to make my own appointment by myself, and I'm going to tell somebody the truth finally.*"

Telling the truth was a major turning point, but the violence against Jane and her son only continued. Her son's mental health was severely impacted. It was only when her abuser began having an affair with a business associate that he made the decision himself to leave. But he fought Jane for custody.

"I had no money. I lost everything, except a house in the middle of the ghetto that I had," she says. Her abuser's financial resources were substantial. "I was forced to give him joint custody of my son."

But her ex's abusive behavior toward their son eventually landed him in jail. The terrible series of incidents that followed created a powerful catalyst for change and gave Jane the opportunity to seek help for herself and for her son.

"Something happened inside of me—I just couldn't give up. And that's how I got involved with the domestic violence organization. That's how I got in with crime victims' advocates. My son went into counseling for almost two years with a specialist in children's issues. I got in domestic violence therapy, domestic violence meetings. I got active in domestic violence, helping at the house that the women were in, and it changed my life."

Jane had returned to the same job where she'd been her entire adult life, earning the same salary as before. A few months in, she had an epiphany. "All the women there were complaining about how they didn't want to do this, didn't want to do that. So I sent emails around asking what would make this office work better. I put a package together, suggested improvements, and presented it to the managing partner. They implemented everything I said. I had lived in survival mode for so long that I had forgotten how smart I really was in thinking logically. And I said to myself, *Damn, I'd forgotten how smart I am. I'm going back to school.*"

Her domestic violence counselor directed Jane to WISP.

"The application process was healing. Writing the essay helped to set me free. It was an expression of defeat, survival, and success. My powerful moment of clarity came when I realized pursuing my education could provide a better life for us. It was an important part in the healing process for me to grow. Receiving the financial aid from WISP gave me the faith and the courage to know that someone believed in me and that I was worthy of more," she says. "And then when I did get the funds, it did something for my self-esteem. I felt seen. It touched my heart and soul; it empowered me to move forward."

Adjusting to life as a student was tough. She was the oldest student in her classes and confounded by the technology. Following her professor's advice, she decided she'd communicate in the way that suited her best—and she'd adopt the mindset that she had something valuable to contribute to the younger students. "I went in there with the attitude of *I can learn from them, and they can learn from me.*" Because of her openness, she was able to forge supportive connections with students, staff, and faculty alike.

The academic work was challenging, but as Jane put it: "I was on a mission, honey. I was on this mission, and you could not have gotten me off this mission with a million dollars. I got it in my head somewhere, *Okay, focus. There's three things you need to pick: God, your son, and your career.* And nobody got in my way."

Her mission demanded sacrifice. "I used every bit of my vacation time. I used my sick time. I wouldn't get paid. I would go to school at night. And I got a lot of Bs and Cs. When you're working full time and you're a single parent, those grades were like golden stars to me," she says. "By the time I graduated, my hair was falling out. I had gained weight. I was eating junk, but I didn't care."

Her graduation day was a proud moment she shared with those who had helped her along the way—including her son and her domestic violence counselor, who were in attendance. She was even singled out by a TV news crew to be interviewed because she was a nontraditional student. She laughs at the memory, knowing her hair and makeup were hardly "camera ready" at that moment. But she leaned into her joy. "I graduated. I walked. I had to be the oldest one there. I've got pictures. I cried through the entire ceremony. I cried like a baby," she says. "Then we had a big party."

Today, she's happy at work and she holds out passing her CPA exam as a future goal. But her education is already having an impact.

"I knew that the only way I was ever going to make any more money than I was making was to educate myself," she says. "That money [from WISP] and getting empowered, empowered me to start researching things like *How do you ask for a raise?* Men have no problem with telling you what they think about themselves," she says. Women, she realized, tend to think they're not good enough. They assume that with hard work and loyalty, they'll be rewarded financially. But often that doesn't happen. "No, you go in there and you have to tell them who you are and what you do for the company," she says. By asking for a raise, Jane now earns a junior partner salary. But she's gotten more than just a bigger paycheck. "Getting the degree and getting the position and making more money is really not all of it. The sense of accomplishment of saying I did it. The wholeness and completion of just knowing that I was capable of being more. And by doing all those things, it helped me start learning how to love myself."

Talking about past experiences is painful, and Jane has found a way to reconcile the pain.

"There's a self-forgiveness. Just forgiving ourselves, accepting and embracing the thought, *What am I going to do with this now?*"

And she knows she is a living testament to what is possible.

"If I survived domestic violence, I can do anything. The sky's the limit. I can do whatever I say I want to do," she says. She knew she had a choice: "Am I going to let this destroy me or am I going to pick up and run with it? Just run with it and see where it takes us. Pain is a great motivator. It was the big motivator in me doing a lot of things that I did, and it forced me not to settle, to never give up no matter what it looked like."

"When you hear somebody else say, *I walked through hell and back, and I'm here to tell about it*, you think, *Maybe I can do that too*," she says. And that's Jane's reason for telling her story. To share what's possible and show others they can do anything they set their minds to.

A Redemption Song

Gloria's Story

WHEN GLORIA EARNED HER BACHELOR's degree in music, she went beyond the traditional student procession. "I danced across the stage. And I got a hug from everybody up there. They put me in the paper, in the magazine. I have a picture of me with my arms in the air, dancing across the stage."

It was truly a dream come true, and a moment that was a long time in coming: Gloria was sixty-two years old. It's an accomplishment she's proud of—and rightfully so—and one that she talks about with others every chance she gets.

Going back to school was something she had wanted to do for years. But when Gloria was in a relationship, her partner's combination of mental illness and personal jealousy made her life a nightmare.

"He was jealous that I had been in college before, and he was jealous of the talent that I have."

Gloria had something that he wanted, and he did everything he could to take it from her. "I told him one day, after five years of being in the marriage, *If you're trying to take my soul, you won't get it. You can't take my soul because it's here in me.* And he started choking me just because I said that. He loved to put fear in me, so I can't think, so I can't be me."

Gloria's yearnings for what her marriage could be come through in the lyrics for her song "Aye":

In a favorite restaurant, see people staring.
What a nice couple, then they're smiling.
Driving through the countryside,
Hear birds all singing.
Flowers blooming everywhere,
And wind blowing through my hair,
Your eyes are smiling.

"I can look back and say that there were times when he would act like a real husband is supposed to act and do the things that husbands are supposed to do. But he was bipolar, and he was schizophrenic, and he didn't believe in Jesus. I didn't know that until after I got married to him. And after eighteen years of struggling, thinking it's going to get better, it got worse and worse."

The abuse often turned violent. Gloria recalls being hit, choked, and even clocked with an iron.

"I thought he was going out of his mind. He hit me over the head twice, saying, *Well, I started now, so I guess I'll finish.* And I thought I was going to die that night. I knew it was time. That was it. And then I had to save my dog, too, because he would have killed her."

Gloria made the decision to walk out the door and cut her abuser out of her life for good.

"I had to tell him that I was going to the store. In June it'll be eleven years that I've been at the store." Gloria is funny. Even when it comes to having to lie and stuff her purse with a toothbrush and other necessities in order to save her life. It's not funny, but she has a way of making it so. Making people laugh and being silly is something that delights Gloria. "I love my sense of humor, and I don't see how anybody can go through life not smiling, with no sense of humor."

It was a difficult road forward. Gloria stayed first with a relative, then at a shelter, and then in transitional housing.

"They teach you how to live by yourself and take care of yourself again," she says. "I had to find me again because I lost me. When I left him, I was so confused and broken, very broken. And I knew I didn't deserve anything like that."

In abusive relationships, that sense of deservedness can get lost. But somewhere, inside, Gloria held on to that. She attributes that to her upbringing.

"I grew up in love. I was the only child. I guess you could say I was a little spoiled brat. But it was all in love."

And to know Gloria is to know that love. She radiates it. People are attracted to her because of it. "Everybody at school was in love with me. Oh my goodness. I would walk in the building, the music building. I would just say, *Hey!* I had a few of them saying it too. *Heyyyy!*"

Gloria had always loved music and had been composing and writing original songs. It was during her time in the transitional housing program that she decided that it was finally time to finish her bachelor's in music. WISP helped her to go back to college, something her abusive ex prevented her from doing during their marriage.

"That was something that I wanted to do for years, and I didn't get a chance to do it until then. But there's a time for everything. And it was time." Gloria knew this was likely her last chance to make her college dreams come true. "I don't see another chance of school in my lifetime. Going back to school was the best thing I could have done to repair some of the brokenness that was bestowed upon me. This helped me to love me for who I am."

At sixty-two, she attracted a lot of attention from other students. But even with the warm reception, Gloria found going back to school a challenge. A degree in music requires a heavy course load, and Gloria took on twelve-plus credits every semester. The transitional housing program sponsored Gloria for WISP, providing needed emotional support as well as the means to receive funds intended to remove barriers to education. Gloria didn't work while she took classes, so the funds WISP provided were her only source of income while she was in school.

"That last semester, oh my God, I cried so much. I was literally bawling, *I can't do this. Please, Lord, I need help. I need help.* But I did it," she says. Gloria says it's partly stubbornness that got her to that graduation stage, and attributes that quality to her parents. "Thanks to my mother and my father, I'm a very determined person. And I will stay a determined person. That's why I graduated."

Since her graduation, Gloria has done a variety of things to help others. As she says: "It's just in my nature. I love helping people. I love to make people smile." By sharing her talents, she's been able to create the peaceful, music-filled life she'd always wanted.

She went on the trip of a lifetime to Poland and Germany to sing with her school's choir. "I felt like a missionary lady. What a blessing!"

She taught beginner's piano to young children for a few years. She's picked up part-time jobs and volunteered for an organization that helps the homeless. To give back to her community, she's participated in seminars and written articles about her experiences for her local paper.

She's also taken the step to copyright her songs. "I want to get them published, so I'm working on that now." She wasn't able to salvage all the music she'd created during her marriage. Most of her works were lost when she made the decision to walk away from her abuser. "It's only three songs that I was able to save. All the rest of them, they're gone. But that's okay. That's all right. God took care of me."

She still sees the therapist she started to work with when she relocated. Although it's been years since she left her husband, his insults and criticisms still haunt her at times. Therapy helps her release the anxiety, and as she says, "I'm still working on me. I'm a work in progress. That was a journey. And I'm still looking for me."

To anyone stuck in an abusive relationship and looking for a way out, Gloria says, "If you want to succeed in leaving with your life, you should plan a safe way to do it. My motto is *You don't plan to fail, you fail to plan.* First of all, believe that God will guide you through it."

Gloria holds herself as a role model and leads by example, showing others that "you can do it; you are worth it; you are somebody; and you are loved."

And if anyone knows about love, it's Gloria.

Speaking Truth to Power

Melonie's Story

COME HELL OR HIGH WATER, Melonie and her megaphone are going to change the world. And she knows it.

"I have nothing to fear anymore because I did it," she says. "I beat the fear of somebody else controlling what I feel because I have control of what I feel, period. I'm pretty bold."

But it was a long road to this realization. For years, Melonie endured abuse by her husband—but she lacked the understanding and context to name the violence she was experiencing.

"I was married to my husband for fifteen years, and we were married for quite a while before I had children. The abuse started almost immediately, but I didn't know any of the red flags—any of the signs—because I was never really educated on it. I grew up in a small town and met him at a military base. Being young and stupid and twenty-one, I didn't realize that he was crossing boundaries. He started isolating me from my friends and family. He moved me away to a completely different state. He started to physically abuse me before we even had children. And I didn't know sex wasn't rape until after I was divorced. It was tumultuous all the way through."

Melonie's mindset offers a powerful insight to others who may not understand why women fail to leave at the first sign of domestic violence. What looks like a bad decision to someone on the outside makes a lot of sense to the person in the situation.

"There were times when the police were called. He beat me enough to where he broke my bones. I left him at one point and told everybody that he had broken my bones. I went back after that and he wouldn't let me get medical treatment. To this day, I have issues with my body because I wasn't able to be properly cared for back then."

But even when she perceived the problem, she faced what many domestic violence victims experience: Leaving was harder than it looked.

"I was going to domestic violence shelters to try and get through a weekend without being beaten in front of my kids. The last domestic violence shelter I was in had bullet holes in the window. I decided it was safer for my children for me to go home and be beaten than it was for me to be in the shelter with these beautiful little people who were one and three. So it just wasn't worth it for me. I knew I made a conscious choice to go back at that point, and I didn't really have any friends I could tell or any family I could share this with."

It took more than one attempt, but she finally left for good. Melonie moved with her children back to her mother's home. And all three started counseling. But danger followed them. Her abuser moved to the town in which she was living and began court proceedings to secure custody.

"He actually ended up taking the kids away from me," she says. She was able to find an attorney with the help of her domestic violence shelter, but that didn't make up for the fact that her abuser had significant social and professional status in their community. It's a special kind of heartbreak for a mother to lose custody of her children to an abuser. Melonie's children stopped speaking to her and she believed it was safer for them that way—to be on his side. She lives with the pain of this loss daily. "He took away my most precious possession," she says. "He has money. He has power. I lost custody."

Still, Melonie was able to tap into the resources of the domestic violence shelter to help her move forward.

"I knew I was healing. Even when I was sitting in there with my children, going to counseling, I was reading books on domestic violence, and I was educating myself, and the counselors would get to know me."

They encouraged Melonie to be part of a twelve-step program called the HEART Program—short for Help End Abusive Relationship Tendencies—to learn to break the abusive relationship cycle. "It was geared toward not ever getting back with that same dude, right? Because that's kind of what you don't ever want to do once you escape. I didn't realize that I was taking back all my power and I was building myself up and changing me."

A friend encouraged Melonie to prioritize herself and suggested she check out the local community college. And when talking to her counselor about this visit, she first heard about WISP. For the first time, Melonie began to think about what she wanted from her life.

The counselor asked her, "What do you want to be when you grow up?"

"And I said, *Well, I don't know. Domestic violence something. I got to change the world because I can't let my daughter go into a domestic violence shelter with bullet holes in the windows ever.*"

WISP made it possible for Melonie to meet her basic needs while in school. She chose social work as a major and completed her associate's degree. That's when she turned her efforts to advocacy. It's when Melonie picked up her megaphone.

"I started my YouTube channel called *Fear You Don't Own Me!* to not only help me personally but, more importantly, help others talk about domestic violence and eventually build domestic violence shelters! I attempt to face my fears head-on while educating others about domestic violence. I am also bringing awareness to domestic violence issues," she says. Melonie had a long list of fears, even including everyday acts such as going outside. "A lot of my videos are about me facing my fears. And at first, I really hated it. And then I get through it and I think, *I just rode in a race car around the track for three laps. Like, what? I went two hundred and twenty miles per hour and looked cute in that helmet.* So yeah, it ended up like an adventure."

It was when her ex-husband was on trial for the rape and murder of another woman that Melonie went beyond her YouTube efforts. He pled guilty and received two years of felony probation. She picketed and protested outside her abuser's employer to bring attention to the way power and money influence domestic violence situations. "I was one of four women testifying. I was silenced in court because of his plea deal, but I could still protest." At first, it was just her. But her one-woman movement is gaining momentum and others are starting to join her efforts. "If there are ten people there with a megaphone and people carrying signs, then maybe, just maybe, the media might get it finally," she says. She leverages her social media account to publicize her efforts—because she's adamant that violent offenders should not be in positions of power over others. And she relishes the way in which she is able to turn the tables. "It organically ended up being where I had a position of power over my abuser, which is what I've got right now. And it's a biggie. It's not a little bit of power. I have it all."

Melonie says it was her education that helped her gain the confidence and skills to evolve from domestic violence victim into her role as an outspoken advocate.

"I could have never had the ability to advocate for others had I not had the education I received. I believe I thrive now because Doris Buffett had this incredible opportunity. Not only did the WISP scholarship change my life and helped me out of domestic violence, but I am most thankful that my education is also helping others."

And she is adjusting to a life in which she can prioritize her own needs.

"It's bizarre to feel happy. Happy makes me cry, which is strange. I don't know how to handle it. I don't know how to grocery shop because I'd always bought for my kids. Who am I? Who is this? I have no idea what to buy. I don't even watch TV because it's like I don't know what to watch. I've watched the kids' stuff. All this is very new. It's all very weird. Happy feels unusual, but it's pretty great and amazing and phenomenal as well. And it's unexplainable what joy feels like, because I didn't know what it felt like till recently."

It's a transformation she relishes.

"This was just a very violent, evil human being who tried to tear me down, but: *Oopsie! Wrong chick, guy!*" she says. "And the future holds what it holds. I really have no control over anything except for being happy. And

I choose happy from the second my feet hit the floor till the time I go to sleep because I've had enough of the pain."

From terrified to triumphant, Melonie's story is about the power of education.

Set Free

Lynda's Story

WHEN LYNDA SPEAKS TO nursing students about job opportunities, she always encourages them to think about their options.

"I tell them they don't have to just go the clinic route," she says. From her own experience in the field, she knows that there's a global path for nurses, too, and it may take you to places and situations you never imagined.

Lynda traveled that global path. But she didn't get there in the way she expected.

When she was a little girl, she did not dream of being a nurse. In fact, the last childhood dream job she can remember was zookeeper, traveling to Africa and working with exotic animals. But as an adult, nursing presented itself as a vocation that worked well with her natural abilities.

"One of my girlfriends advised me, *You should be a nurse*," Lynda says. The friend pointed out that Lynda is always on the scene to help someone who is hurt—even to help animals in need. "She herself was a very accomplished nurse and hugely respected on our island for a lot of her work." That advice had a strong impact on Lynda's thinking.

When Lynda found herself entangled in a twelve-year marriage in which her husband abused her physically, verbally, and emotionally, nursing began to take shape as a way out. "I got this bright idea: *That's how I'm going to escape this relationship. I'm going to be a nurse.*"

And she was determined to make that happen, no matter what. It was one day while riding with her husband in their truck that she made her bold move.

"We're in the truck and I say, *Hey, pull into the college.*" Her husband responded as he often did, criticizing her, telling her she was too stupid to go to college. He drove onto the grounds anyway. But when he realized his words were not going to deter Lynda, he lashed out. "We pull into the college, and I go to get out of the truck, and he panics because he realizes it's one more thing I'm going to do to get away. He grabs the back of my head and slams it into the doorjamb."

Lynda got away and made her way toward the entrance. "So I walk into college—no appointment—and my eye is swelling up."

Undeterred, she asked for the nursing department and followed the instructions down the hall. "I go in and sit down. I've got this growing lump on my head. And I say, *I want to join.* And she looks at me and says, *Um, this is college. We don't join. We register.*"

But the interview continued, and the college administrator asked Lynda about her background. "I told her I'm self-taught. I grew up with hippies. I'm very well read. I know a lot about history. I can write. I'm listing all the things I can do. And I'm trying to avoid the fact that I didn't graduate from high school."

But after a few moments, the interview took a different turn.

"She looks at me and she says, *What is wrong with your head?* And I start bawling and the whole story comes tumbling out. And I say, *Oh, my gosh. And he's out in the car, and he's telling me I'm stupid, and I've been dealing with this for years.*"

Lynda recalls the college administrator listening carefully to the entire story. Then she spoke up: "You say you can write? Here's an address. Write them a story about what you just told me."

The address was for WISP. And Lynda was taking the first step in securing the funds and the support she'd need to pursue a nursing degree. When she got the award letter, she cried. "You guys accepted me. I was up against a wall when I got that scholarship," she says. "Every time I'd get a letter from you guys, I was so excited. I had a whole file. I'd save it all, and you guys would send me these funny little letters congratulating me whenever I got good grades."

In nursing school, Lynda faced a steep learning curve. Not only did she need to learn who Warren and Doris Buffett were, she had to fill in the gaps in her self-taught education. She needed classes in remedial math to catch up. She had to adapt to a more formal schooling process. But once again, she was determined to make this opportunity work.

"I was the oldest one in nursing school. I took it seriously. I needed to change my life. I could not walk down the street in our tropical paradise town and compete for a tourist job with twenty-one-year-olds. I couldn't do that. I had four kids."

But in nursing school, Lynda quickly saw results.

"I was a straight-A student throughout my entire schooling. I was president of Phi Theta Kappa. I made the dean's list. All these things were so empowering to me after living with him for so long, and just being told, you're stupid, you're ugly, you're fat," she says. "I got my first A on a paper. It was a really difficult class. I remember running straight to the payphone with my quarters, calling my girlfriend, who got me into this, and I'm crying on the phone on campus, *I got an A! I got an A!* And she says, *Of course you did!*" All these elements combined to help rebuild the self-esteem Lynda had seen eroded during her marriage.

Still, nursing school was difficult, and not just academically. Lynda encountered critiques of her appearance reminiscent of the control her abuser exerted. This time, though, she pushed back.

"We live in the tropics," Lynda says. "And nursing instructors are very conservative. They weren't nice," she says. She found the focus on her appearance to be misplaced. "I just kept telling them, *Hey, I'm going to be a good nurse. I'm here in this college paying you to educate me. You don't tell me what I should dress like.*"

She had one memorable run-in with a faculty member. "I was walking through school one day in a typical outfit. I probably had platform shoes on. I probably had a short skirt on and something not inappropriate by any means, but by her standards it was. She had said something about my outfit and I turned around in the courtyard, filled with people because it was a break time. I looked at her and I said, *You know what, I'm going to be a great nurse one day.* And she waited for me to turn around and yelled out in front of everybody, *You will never be a good nurse if you continue to dress like a streetwalker.*"

It wasn't a surprise to Lynda. "These ladies did not like me. I was not their cup of tea."

But she pushed on. Nothing the nursing instructors could say or do was worse than the abuse she endured in her marriage, and having broken free of that—no one was going to tell her what she could or could not do. "I'm not going to stop being who I am. I had somebody erasing me for twelve years in that relationship. I'll never erase myself for anyone else ever again."

Even with the support of a scholarship, she needed to work. At one point, she was the only female deck hand on a fishing boat.

"My captain was the most abusive thing you could possibly imagine. I would leave the dock at five in the morning with this guy who just abused me verbally. So while watching those lures, I would think to myself, *You can bitch at me all day long to the back of my head while I'm working to pay for nursing school, and it's not as bad as it was at home.*"

Anytime Lynda encountered abuse, she would tough it out or even push back, thinking of all she'd already overcome. "I was like a bird let out of the cage. I'm not flying back. I'm out of that cage. You guys can dish it out all day long. You don't know what I've been going through for the last twelve years." She'd been set free.

She had her heart set on working for Doctors Without Borders, known by its French name *Médecins Sans Frontières* (MSF). Many told her over the years that her global aspirations were impossible, but she never gave up. Upon graduating, she stacked up the experience she needed to turn that dream into a reality.

"Right after I graduated, I went and got my surgery experience first. And straight after that, I went with an organization to Africa. And I lived in Kenya for eight months in a mud hut in a community with a seventy-eight percent positive HIV/AIDS rate," she says. "Being a Caucasian woman, and from America, and with a degree, I was made medical director of the unit, which was ridiculous. I had zero skills for that. I learned a lot. I stayed there for eight months. I absolutely love that village."

With those experiences under her belt, she was ready for the next step. It took persistence, grit, and a little bit of luck, but she landed a contract with *Médecins Sans Frontières* and took her first assignment in Nigeria. "I worked on an abused women's surgical unit where they do vesicovaginal fistula repair. The need there was heartbreaking," she says. "These poor girls, they're nine, ten, eleven years old when they develop their fistulas because their sixty-year-old husband got them pregnant." The physical trauma of these pregnancies and childbirth often leaves the young girls incontinent and shunned by family members. "So they throw them outside the hut with the dog. They can't get rid of them, so they put them outside with the animals." MSF provided surgical repairs, months of rehabilitation, and skills training.

Lynda took another position in Haiti after the devastating earthquake there. After her three-month assignment, she left. She was on the road home when, back in the US, news organizations were reporting the kidnapping of American MSF women in Haiti. It was Lynda's replacement who was taken. However, Lynda's adult children in the US endured a stressful period of days in which they did not know if it was Lynda or not.

"When I got home, they had a sit-down and said, *Mom, can you think about getting a normal job like everybody else's mom?*"

She took a corporate job and has been with the company for twelve years. It was an adjustment. "You are definitely in a checklist-manifesto world. Check the box, check the box. Very corporate. They have a lot of liability. Adjusting to that environment was another learning experience. I remember my first interview, the nursing supervisor of our section said, *We're just afraid you're going to want to spread your wings.* And I said, *No, I'm a pretty humble being. I've done a lot of spiritual work and I've been through a lot and I'm ready to just step in and be a team player,*" she says.

She reflects on her experiences: "All my life I've been an adrenaline junkie. As much as I wanted to want to go out in the field and be a nurse and save people, the fact is—they saved me. Every single patient along the way has saved me, taught me something, and brought growth in my life. You see people at their absolute worst, and it helps you realize your woes aren't that big." And although nursing was not her original career plan, it fulfilled her childhood wishes. "I did go to Africa. I did see all those zoo animals."

She's often asked to speak about her experiences as a domestic abuse survivor, but she chooses those options carefully. She's mindful that her physical appearance—white, blonde, tall—may have afforded her some measure of privilege that other women may not have. But she also realizes that she has the ability to connect with audiences and spread a message.

"I don't typify the abused woman," she says. When she speaks about her past, she can see the way faces change in the audience and how they react to her story. She's gratified that her speaking can help others raise funds to help battle domestic violence.

Ultimately, Lynda sees that the people she's encountered and the experiences she's had—both positive and negative—led her to where she is today, and her message is one of gratitude. When she looks around her beautiful home, she says, with some degree of astonishment, "I wouldn't be here without the scholarship. I'm a nurse. I get a paycheck. I can pay for my own things. I have insurance. I did everything I wanted to do. Dreams fulfilled. Nursing changed my life. You guys changed my life."

Lynda's story reminds us of the power of community. "I just feel like my safety net was woven out of people spread out like starfish, all holding hands and feet together under me. WISP, my girlfriend, the microbiology professor, my kids. I can never fall because I don't have it in me. But if I did, you guys were all there."

Forging a New Path

Elvira's Story

FOR ELVIRA, the drive to break the generational cycles of single motherhood and poverty powers her efforts. The past does not dictate the future, she tells herself, her daughters, and so many in her community. But even when you know that truth, she says, breaking the cycle is hard.

"I was named after my mom. I feel like I carry her trauma, and it's on me to change that narrative that people always think about us," she says. "They say, *Okay, because she was a drug addict and she had ten children, that all of her children weren't going to be anything.* And because I was her first girl, they said, *What makes her think that she's not going to turn out to be a drug addict?*" Elvira felt their judgment and their assumptions that she, too, would follow the same path her mother took. "And I said, *No, I'm going to change the narrative.*"

Even that came with judgment, she says. "They said, *Now she thinks she's better than us.* And I said, *No, it's because I want better for me. And you could do the same if you put your mind to it.* It's just that simple. But because of where we come from, because of the stereotype, because of the environment, they think they can't. But I told my kids, *We're not the product of our environment, so if we want change, we have to be the change that we're looking for.*"

It's this internal drive to better her own life and the lives around her that inspires Elvira even in difficult times.

Elvira's childhood was turbulent. Her family lacked the money to provide the basics for Elvira and her siblings. Her father, a Cuban immigrant, did his best to provide for his children despite his own lack of education and difficulty securing work.

"We were living in such horrible conditions. No lights. We were washing up outside at the fire hydrants. We had soap and we washed up with our clothes on. I'm eight years old. I didn't really think nothing of it."

But the authorities were less accepting. Elvira and her siblings were removed from the family and put into foster care. Elvira was quickly separated from her brothers, who went to another family. And then her own foster family decided they could only keep one child, so Elvira's sister was placed elsewhere. "Oh my God, I just felt alone," Elvira recalls.

Instability characterized her childhood experiences, moving from foster home to foster home. The system failed to protect her from sexual abuse and failed to help her father in his efforts to reunite the family.

One of her foster parents tried to help. "She said to me, *Elvira, I do care about you. I do want you to do what you need to do. You're capable of doing everything that you need to do. You're using your situation. You don't have to be like this.* But I was twelve, a very stubborn kid. I said, *You guys don't love me. You don't know me. You all don't want the best for me. You all just want the money.* That's how I was looking at it."

Elvira was not ready to hear that message. She ran away from her foster home several times. When she turned sixteen, she emancipated herself, escaping from a system she'd grown tired of, knowing it wouldn't give her the safety and stability she needed.

As a teenager, she struggled to escape the pull of her generational history. "I met this boy, and he was whispering sweet nothings. He was eighteen and telling me, *Everything's going to be okay.* And boom. I got pregnant."

Elvira was now a young mother with no template for motherhood. Despite pressure to terminate her pregnancy, Elvira's stubbornness became a strength, and she made her first moves toward independence and creating a better life for herself and her baby. "I said, *I'm not getting rid of it. I'm going to keep it, and I'm going to be the best mother that I can be.*"

Her father had often spoken of the value of education, saying it was the key to getting out of poverty. His words now returned to help Elvira shape a new plan. "I enrolled in night school. I was working at McDonald's. I went to school with night class, and I worked in the daytime." She had moved in with the baby's father but was dismayed that he was continuing his own pattern of selling drugs, and he wasn't supportive of her going to school. "My whole mindset just changed. I wanted better. And then when I knew my baby was a girl I thought, *She needs to be in a better environment.* I graduated from night school with my high school diploma, and then I went to community college." At her young age, Elvira already knew that she wanted to be a nurse. She had an innate need to help others. So she kept up her studies at the community college to bring herself closer to that goal.

Her first child was nearing the age of three when Elvira met and married a man with plans for a career in the military. She had two children with him, and when he was stationed stateside, Elvira continued her quest for further education, adding a certification in phlebotomy to her credentials. But everything changed when her husband was sent to Iraq and came back traumatized by the experience. His behavior disrupted the marriage and Elvira's plans to create a stable home for herself and her children.

"He had trauma, but at the same time, his mother just didn't make situations better. I was always the one in the middle. And he started to cheat."

Elvira tried to manage the situation but found herself overwhelmed by the demands of three young children and a husband who often was not around. She was shocked when she found her mother-in-law to be of little support. "She said, *Well, that's what men do. Men cheat. You just got to learn to live with it.*"

But Elvira was unwilling to accept that role. She made the decision to leave her husband and take her children to safety—even though it meant going to a shelter. And even though it meant angering her unstable husband.

Initially, she tried living with family. "I packed my stuff up and I moved. He tried to make it so difficult. He wanted us to come back home. He went and told the landlord that I was staying there with my sister. And the landlord told my sister that if I didn't leave, then they would evict her."

So Elvira and her children moved to a shelter—but her husband then tried to use that against her in court. "He took the children from me. He said, *She's homeless. She's living in a shelter.* He was trying to make me feel like the bottom of the barrel." This time, the system didn't fail. The judge was able to see the bigger picture. "The judge said, *Well, why is she going through all this? Is it because of you?*" The truth came out and Elvira's husband was ordered to return the children to her custody and pay child support.

It was at her local shelter that Elvira first found WISP—and the inspiration to continue her education.

WISP was able to give Elvira the financial—and emotional—support she needed to resume her education. She recalls conversations with her WISP contact in which they wouldn't just talk about school or finances, but about Elvira and how she was managing daily life. "WISP was like a ray of sunshine. I was supported financially and spiritually—like family. People I didn't know saw strength in me that I could not see."

Still, the path through higher education was bumpy. First, she did a four-week certified nursing assistant class and got a job. She started school for her licensed practical nursing degree (LPN) but had difficulty adapting to that school's educational style. "They made me feel like I just couldn't do it. They weren't supportive."

She withdrew and moved. She was accepted into a Habitat for Humanity program and worked toward her dream of owning a home. It was difficult, especially restoring her ruined credit. Her ex failed to pay for a car that was in her name, and she ended up with a black mark on her credit report. "They said, *You have to fix your credit.* Everything that was on a checklist, I did it. I crossed it off, one thing at a time. I said, *Elvira, you can do this. If anybody else could do this, you can do this.* I said, *We need this house of ours for the kids. It's for stability. That's what you're longing for—stability.*"

In the midst of working toward homeownership, life took another un-expected turn. Elvira discovered she was pregnant with her fourth child. This could have derailed her housing plans, and at first, her sister was going to adopt the baby. But Elvira changed her mind. She'd gotten this far with three children, and she decided she'd keep doing it with four. Although the timing made it tough, she signed the lease on her new home, and the baby came soon after.

With her housing situation stabilized, it was finally time for Elvira to return to school. She went back to finish her LPN—this time at a school with an educational philosophy that suited her learning style. "We did a lot of hands-on. They understood that people learned in different ways. They didn't just give you a bunch of essays and stuff to do. They really worked with you, and they were really supportive." And WISP was there to help her finish what she started.

"And then I passed the LPN program. I was walking on the stage. It was like a breath of fresh air. I thought, *Elvira, you did it. You did it!*"

Elvira found her niche in working with the elderly community. After two decades in the industry, however, she realized that nursing was no longer fulfilling her inner passion to care for people. And so, she's found another way to channel her gift for taking care of others.

She's finishing a program in massage therapy. She has a job offer waiting for her at graduation, and she has plans to go into business with her daughters—all three of whom have cosmetology degrees.

Elvira notes there's often cultural pressure to stay small rather than dream big. "The society we live in has plateaued. Everybody's comfortable work-ing at McDonald's and all this kind of stuff, so they want me to stay put. *You make X amount of money. Why can't you just stay and be a nurse?*" But Elvira wants more. "That's not where I'm happy at. I don't care about how much I'm making. I care about everything in general. I want to be happy," she says. "I'm nervous. I'm super nervous. This is something for me, too, but at the same time, I'm not going to doubt my ability of what I can do." The self-doubt is there, but Elvira's desire to spread her wings is stronger, and she knows that this is the move that will bring her closer to doing work that brings her joy. "Caring for people is my thing," she says.

Even as she moves into this new career path, life is never simple. Elvira is a grandmother now—a status she took some time to accept since it meant her daughter was following her footsteps into single motherhood—a cycle Elvira hoped to break. "At first, I was very upset. I was like, *Oh my God, this was not part of the plan.*" But she's seeing a greater blessing now. "And then I was thinking about it. I said, *You know what? My life wasn't a part of the plan either.*"

If the plan for Elvira's life was to follow in her mother's footsteps, then she has certainly broken that mold.

"When my mom passed away, I was going to push the school thing back. And then I said, *No, that's not what she would have wanted for me. I need to go harder. Start the new chapter in my career and move forward with that. I don't know how I'm going to do it. But I figured it out this far,*" she says. "You've got to put in the work because it's all about consistency. Consistency is everything. And you got to keep going, keep going, keep going. You'll get there. I don't care if you're like a turtle or a worm, you'll get there. The only thing that can stop you is yourself."

Elvira didn't have a road map for life so she made one. Her story is a reminder: Don't let anything hold you back from doing what brings you satisfaction and joy.

Women Helping Women

Carrie's Story

"I just knew I wanted a different life."

It wasn't a plan any more complicated or fleshed out than that simple statement. But Carrie felt it keenly and held on to it.

Looking back, Carrie can see she's been in abusive relationships all her life. But it was the one she entered in her early forties that put her in the most danger.

"I had gotten into a relationship with a very bad man. I started misusing my ADHD medication to cope. He was a drug user and that spiraled into my addiction to methamphetamines. It was a coping mechanism. Not a healthy coping mechanism, but it was the only one that I had at the time," she recalls.

Carrie was arrested on a minor drug charge and jailed for several months. It was during that time that she had her simple but clear vision: She wanted a different life.

But it was not a straight line to that outcome.

While she was out on probation, her ex began stalking her, unwilling to let her move forward with her life. And he was willing to use violence to stop her.

First, he broke her nose. Worried about her safety, her probation officer forbade Carrie to see him anymore. But he continued to apply pressure and worm his way into Carrie's life.

It was only a month later that he injured her again—this time leaving her with staples in her scalp.

But since Carrie's probation officer had told her not to see her ex, this injury came with a legal—and ultimately helpful—outcome. The fact that Carrie had been in contact with her ex was a violation of her probation, and Carrie found herself before a judge. The judge had the same concerns as the probation officer: Carrie's ex was a serious threat to her life.

"The judge said, *If we allow you to get out of jail, we're going to be reading your obituary. He's going to kill you,*" Carrie recalls.

So Carrie went back to jail. She was in custody for six months. When she got out, as luck would have it, her abusive ex had landed behind bars. That gave Carrie the open space to put her plan for a different life into motion.

While incarcerated, Carrie had taken advantage of classes and support groups designed to aid women battling addiction and dealing with domestic abuse. After her release, she spent several months at a sober house and then pursued a spot in a residential program for survivors of domestic violence. She sat on the waitlist for months, diligently calling every week to check on her status, before she finally secured a spot. "I just knew that this was a place where I could learn." And she wanted to learn all she could about creating the better life she was after.

It was in this program that a therapist encouraged her to define this "different" life she wanted. "My therapist said, *What do you want to do with your life?* And I said, *I want to go back to school and maybe do what you're doing.* And she said, *I think you should absolutely do that.* And so that was when I decided to go back to school."

The therapist connected Carrie with WISP and she was accepted into the program. WISP underwrote her associate's degree. Then her bachelor's in social work.

"WISP lovingly supported me all the way through my undergrad," she says. "Not only was the money very helpful for me, but I don't know if I could have gotten through school without that extra help. All the loving support that you gave me personally and just those little extra bits of encouragement—the little books that you sent and the encouraging words. I think that my experience would have been very different without you all."

Carrie finished her BSW in 2020 and then, on her own, continued her education and earned her master's in social work.

For Carrie, going back to school in her forties was difficult. She wasn't even sure she would be accepted to a program. And then, once there, she had additional hurdles to clear.

"Getting through math—that was a thing. And switching from community college to the 'big school'—how scary is that for me as a nontraditional student, still being on felony probation."

At the same time, Carrie was working to rebuild her relationships with family. "Regaining the trust of my family and my daughter especially, who worried that her mom was going to go back to a man who may repeat these patterns. Rebuilding that trust with her and that relationship and getting to know each other again, all that was happening at the same time." School played a role in that process. "By graduating with that degree, I could say, *Here's another thing that I did that's hopefully going to show you all that I'm serious about this.*"

Another way Carrie demonstrated her seriousness was by addressing her legal history so that the past would not hold her back. "Going through the process of getting off probation early and going through the courts to have my felony reduced to a misdemeanor—that was a milestone. But it meant I wasn't going to have that hanging over my head anymore."

Today, Carrie has come full circle. After a series of internships and jobs, the residential program where she once lived offered her a position. "It's amazing to be here, to be able to say, *Oh, I used to live in that room. I've gone up these stairs with my own therapist.* It's pretty wild to shift to the lens of being a therapist sometimes. I've worked a lot of different jobs in my life. But when I come here, I absolutely feel it's a second home. And not just because I'm here eight hours a day, but because I really do feel like it's where I belong and it's where I am doing the most valuable work in the world," she says.

Here, her past is an asset. "Knowing that I have been a survivor brings a level of nonjudgment and trust."

Looking back, Carrie says she can see she was helped by a community of women helping other women. At the time she was arrested, she couldn't see it as any kind of positive. "My PO knew what she was doing because she did not want me to die. She was a very strong, powerful, frankly terrifying kind of woman, and she was not going to sit by and, on her watch, allow her client to die. And that's very likely where I would have ended up."

The judge Carrie appeared before was also a woman. Again, Carrie recalls it was hard to see the actions of both these women as positive. But she sees it now.

"I do remember feeling like, *Oh, this is cool. I'm getting arrested for getting beat up.* And sitting that very first morning in prison and being asked, *What are you in here for?* I said, *I got beat up one too many times. And so here we are.* It just didn't seem fair. But it didn't take very long for me to figure out. My PO saved my life that day. I've always wanted to thank her. And I haven't yet, but I still think about it every day."

Carrie's experiences have helped her make connections with other women seeking a new life after domestic violence. "Knowing how I struggled with my own identity after abuse, I recognize that many of my clients are just beginning to explore who they are after escaping a controlling partner. I think that being able to show up for women in the most authentic way possible is very valuable. From the way my office is decorated, to the clothes I wear. I can't pretend to be someone I am not, and I want my clients to be comfortable with who they are in that space. When we can show up as our most genuine, authentic selves, I think that really comes through with our clients."

She's even referred other women to WISP.

"When I was facilitating NA groups in a hospital, I met a gal there who was having some problems. I told her about the residential program, and I told her about WISP. And then she ended up coming to the domestic violence program and living in the shelter for a while and then going back to school utilizing WISP. She wants to be a social worker too."

This became a theme in Carrie's life, even as she moved through her own education. "I started mentoring women who were coming out of prison to help them reintegrate back into society. I got on the board of the mentoring program to help that program run smoother. Then I got on another advisory board to help the leadership there. I hadn't been in prison very long, but I knew how the system worked with probation and parole. We meet once every two months to talk about their future initiatives. They're going to be building a new women's prison, which sounds awful. But if they're going to have them, why not make them trauma informed? We know that the prisons are full of women who are there because of abusive relationships." It's surprising to realize that prison was rehabilitative for Carrie, and she's doing what she can to make that true for others. It's all about helping women any way she can, she says.

Carrie relishes the different life she has built for herself, recognizing that it wasn't a break from her past, but a reconfiguration of what happened to her. "To be able to go out and to do this type of work, it's really turned this painful part of my life into something that is actually giving me purpose."

The Power of Small Steps

Mary Ann's Story

FOR MARY ANN, highlights come in the form of emails from former students. One sends a note to say she was instrumental in their making a good decision about a future path. Another tells Mary Ann how she helped them find the insight and courage to change course and pivot to a second career.

"I cry a lot when I get those. We're just on our own path and it touches so many others, and it's so rare to see the impact we have," she says.

Mary Ann's path to college instructor and mentor hardly seemed obvious back when she was still mired in her abusive marriage—a relationship that lasted thirty-two years. Leaving was physically dangerous and emotionally difficult. Still, Mary Ann's feisty Celtic warrior roots showed up in her unwillingness to completely submit.

"Even in the midst of the horrific relationship, I still continued to balk, to compete. And that was one of the things that drove my ex crazy—the fact that I wouldn't lie down and roll over," she says. "There was always something that I could do better or faster than he could. It drove him nuts."

And looking back, Mary Ann—all four feet ten inches of her—feels some satisfaction in having been able to fight back in her own kind of way. But this relationship was not a game, and Mary Ann came to realize the physical threat she faced. "I took up martial arts because I was threatened.

It was very disconcerting to my ex—which was a good thing. This was the point at which I was sleeping with a loaded gun under my pillow."

There was a definitive—and devastating—event that prompted Mary Ann to finally leave.

"The major turning point was the violent death of our older daughter, which was related to the years of domestic violence and abuse. I struggled for a long time with my feelings of being responsible for her death. If I had left him and taken the girls with me, she would still be alive. If I had left, what else would have been different in all of our lives? Guilt is a very tough taskmaster when you think you could have changed the outcome."

She was working with a victim services organization when she first became aware of WISP.

"WISP gave me the ability to accomplish anything I envision doing." It was the support that allowed her to rediscover what she'd heard from her father in childhood: *You can do anything you set your mind to.* It was his belief in her abilities that formed her foundation, and it was to that foundation she returned. "That's where the wheels start turning. And it allows you to start to dream, to create, to envision. There has to kind of be a starting point and realization: *Yes, I can do this.* It starts in small steps."

And for Mary Ann, that first small step was going back to school. Despite a long hiatus from education, the timing seemed perfect.

"I dreamed of finishing what I started in 1968. There was that decades-long gap, and it was the turn of the century, too, because it was around 2001. And I decided this was an opportunity. It's as if the universe said, *This is a whole new century, have at it.*"

But education in this new century presented plenty of challenges. Mary Ann had been absent from the college world for decades and, upon her return, faced a steep learning curve on how to be a twenty-first-century student.

"I had the learning curve of the computers as well as learning the course content and subject matter."

She moved from chemistry to biology before settling on psychology as a major. And she quickly became involved in research.

"I had a lot to prove, particularly to myself, so I was very driven. When I was still an undergrad, I was invited to become part of the research team in filicide." The professor running the research team didn't know her family history. Mary Ann helped conduct the research and build the field's first database. Doing this work was interesting on an intellectual level as well as a personal level. "Filicide is different in that it goes beyond intrafamily violence, aggression, and homicide. It's very specific. And when you have that background of domestic violence, you do want to, I think, have some semblance of an understanding of what it is, why did this set of dynamics evolve? It could have something to do with wondering, *Is it something I did or didn't do?* It starts out that way, out of curiosity. I can't leave things alone; I have to dismantle them. I like to see how they tick."

WISP provided support during Mary Ann's BA in psychology, and she went on to pursue a master's and a PhD on her own. Through the process, she displayed her own unique brand of brilliance and energy, quickly finishing her master's before going into the PhD program.

"I finished the master's degree in four semesters. I don't advise it. That meant all of the courses. It meant the research. It meant writing the master's thesis. It meant defending the thesis. Four semesters. I graduated [with my master's] in December of 2006, and I started my PhD in January of 2007. In two weeks, I went from finishing a master's to starting a doctorate. No pressure!"

Mary Ann is a true polymath. She has a voracious appetite for learning and mastering the topics she's interested in. In this case, she was driven by her own internal need to understand, to know why. In this way, she took an intellectual approach to healing from abuse.

She went to one of the only colleges in the country that offered a PhD in conflict analysis and resolution and crisis management. "I knew that's where I needed to be. I didn't need another degree in psychology. I needed to understand the dynamics of conflict," she says. "One of the interesting lessons about this whole thing is, in all of our training with conflict and crisis management, you not only learn how to manage and sometimes resolve conflict, you learn how to start it. Sometimes you will just be involved in something or you will see something that cannot continue. We are extremely well versed in being able to start the conflict to initiate change."

Understanding how conflict can be used as a catalyst for positive change was the way Mary Ann was able to "flip the script." Conflict could be used as a tool to fix a problem, rather than cause one. Viewing conflict through an entirely different lens allowed Mary Ann to harness her natural inclination to create change even in the most daunting of circumstances.

While making her way through school, she worked in a variety of jobs, from a director at a children's center to the co-owner of an exotic pet store.

"Never much going on at home unless somebody decided to take a vacation outside of their habitat, such as the bearded lizard in the dining room one evening, or the eyelash viper perched in the papasan chair in the lanai," she says. "Never a dull moment. Watch where you're walking and always carry a snake hook!"

But it was the education world that continued to draw her in. She worked as a coordinator for students at East Carolina University. She's frequently involved in creating curricula on topics such as conflict resolution. She even created a student engagement project that she hopes will be part of a NASA education program. Through it all, she's learned the hard way to delegate and prioritize.

"I do have a tendency to keep achieving. Sometimes it's too much of a good thing. It's all positive, but there's a lesson in here which says you can't do it all. As much as you would like to, you have to learn to let go. You have to learn to delegate, sometimes postpone. It's all part of the learning lessons."

Still, that doesn't keep her from taking on new challenges. And she is a force. When she's hot on a project, even contacting the White House isn't out of the question. She'll go toe-to-toe with anyone, and it's likely that she'll win.

"Right now, I'm on a couple of missions. I have contacted the White House to have real estate tax eliminated for widows of one hundred percent disabled veterans who have died due to their service-connected disabilities/injuries. Next, the oldest golf course in my area was devastated by a hurricane last year. I am working on fundraising to purchase and renovate the golf course so it can be used for other types of events and fundraisers. I did not plan on owning a golf course in this lifetime, but I don't plan on seeing the community lose this beautiful green space."

A mission that is especially dear to her heart is the Teddy Bear Project, an organization she founded that gives teddy bears to children experiencing times of major stress, distress, and sadness in an effort to improve their quality of life by providing them with understanding, caring, nurturing, and empathic support.

"The TBP gives me the opportunity to help other children who are abused, neglected, abandoned, and homeless. I feel that my daughter is here with me every step of the way." Soothing the hurts of children through her work with the Teddy Bear Project helps Mary Ann soothe her own wounds.

Her life has come full circle now. She's remarried to the man who was her high school sweetheart. And she lives according to her father's early teachings: You can accomplish anything you want to do.

Even if you have to travel a nontraditional path to get there.

Trust the Process

Masako's Story

LEAVING AN ABUSER is often a process that rolls out in stages. This was Masako's experience as she worked to disengage from the escalating menace of her marriage.

At one point, she left with her young daughter and moved in with a friend who lived on the other side of the state. "It was during summer break, and I told my husband we were staying with my friend and her kids, like a vacation, so he wouldn't get angry or suspicious." But Masako struggled to find work so that she could leave her friend's apartment and live independently.

"I applied at over a hundred and forty places when I was with her for those three months, and I maybe got less than ten interviews. I was just applying, filling out forms, sending my resume and sometimes a picture, and just not hearing anything, ever. It's like I'm lost out there in the ocean of the internet. It was so frustrating."

After several months of searching, and with summer coming to an end, she felt she had no other choice but to go back home—and back to her abusive husband. But the brief absence had one successful outcome. It embedded the idea in Masako's mind that leaving was necessary.

"From there on, it was just planning how I was going to leave him."

And that necessity was only increasing.

"He treated me poorly, and it was almost becoming physical," she says. And Masako knew she'd need to find a better environment for her daughter. "She was getting older, and I could just see how he would transfer it to her. I thought, *That's not going to happen. She's still suffering from some of the trauma of him screaming at me, the police coming because he's going off in a rant or rage.* And he had gotten into drugs and alcohol. It just became a huge problem that was like a fire going out of control. I knew that it was headed in a bad direction."

It was the Christmas season when she made the effort that would finally stick.

"We literally walked away from our home, and I walked away from about eight-five percent of my things. That was really hard. But I remember we walked down the driveway and I was thinking, *Just don't look back, don't look back, don't look back.*"

The aftermath was difficult. Masako's husband took his name off their apartment lease, resulting in an eviction that remains on her record. Her housing situation was chaotic, with mother and daughter moving often between tiny houses and friends' couches. At a domestic violence survivor program, counselors pressed Masako to make a plan.

"They wanted me to make a decision about how I was going to sustain a future life with me and my daughter. And I said, *I want to go to school and become a nurse.* That was something I'd wanted to do when I was married to him. He just was not supportive at the time. So that's what I did—dove right into it."

She quickly discovered securing funds for college would be a challenge. Scholarship money did not always match up with semester bill payments. What's more, since Masako had been to college previously, she was ineligible for many grant programs.

"I don't even remember how I found WISP. But when I found out that a WISP scholarship was renewable, I thought, *Oh my God, you guys just saved me.* I didn't even have to stop. I was able to continue on and get my bachelor's degree along with the RN degree because of WISP," she says. She was astounded that an individual like Doris Buffett would be willing to hand out money in that fashion. "For someone like Doris to do what she did, it's unheard of. I mean, who does that? People just don't do that. For her to give away money and help people in the way that she has, especially single, abused women with children—it saves lives."

In addition to the financial support from WISP, Masako credits the non-monetary support WISP provides, such as contact via text and email and small things that came in the mail. When she was still couch surfing in search of a permanent home, she kept a post office box in which WISP items would sometimes land. She recalls the day she received her acceptance letter from WISP and opened it in her car—sending the trademark WISP gold stars flying everywhere. "I still have stars in my car!"

There were other items from WISP that she treasures. The book of inspirational quotes, a postcard with a butterfly, the biography of Doris Buffett. She's passed many of these objects on to her daughter. And she fondly recalls the Motivational Monday Messages that came via email—ones with words of inspiration. Once, one contained a link to the song "This Is Me" from the movie *The Greatest Showman*. "I was in my car and I put my AirPods in, and I just kept playing it and playing it, and then I started singing it, and I was crying and trembling and shaking. It was both healing and intense."

There have been many hurdles to Masako's education. She began training in her midforties—older than most of her classmates. Just as she was starting to feel comfortable, the COVID pandemic hit. At first, student nurses were banished from the hospitals, making it impossible for Masako to complete her necessary clinical hours. She would have to repeat a semester. Then later in the pandemic, when nurses were burning out, Masako was told she could return to the hospital, but she wondered if it was safe for her daughter and the family she was staying with.

Nursing school on its own is intense. Even more so for a single parent. "School was very difficult. Being a single parent and all the other things I had going on, I had to quit a job to continue school, and finding ways of making money was insane. I was leaning on the state a little bit for help, and whatever I could get my hands on to get us through those situations." In response to a demand for nurses with bachelor's degrees, the community college partnered with a private university to offer a dual enrollment program, where students would be going to both schools simultaneously. It was an additional challenge and a great opportunity. Masako remembers being daunted by the financial toll enrolling in a private school would take. "They said, *You guys can do it!* And oh my God, I was scared. The problem was, being a private college, it was very expensive. I couldn't get grants because I had gone to school prior to this. The situation I was in was just so unique because it was hard to find scholarships that I fit into. I was older, I already had a liberal arts degree. And all of a sudden, I'm out of the game. When I first started doing it, people were saying to me, *You have a degree. You can get a job.* That kind of thing."

Despite all of her concerns, Masako made the leap, enrolled in the program, and earned her bachelor's in nursing.

Then, after she graduated and was on the brink of taking her licensing exam and achieving her goal, a new tragedy shook her: Her ex-husband was murdered—shot numerous times by his roommate.

When she found out what happened, the loss hit hard. Masako had extricated herself from the abuse in the relationship with her ex, but there was no lingering animosity. She'd been able to forge an amicable relationship with her daughter's father, finding forgiveness in knowing that he struggled with his own demons. Though she harbored no illusions that they'd ever reunite, she was at peace with this new way of associating with him and successfully coparenting their daughter. The grief she experienced was complicated, and she had no one in her life who could understand.

"It's such a blur. I had to go empty out his room. I went to the scene where it happened, and they hadn't cleaned up anything. The front door had a big hole in it from the SWAT team. They put pepper spray bombs in the house when they broke in because they didn't know if this guy was going to shoot them. I had to wear the N-95 mask that we were fitted for in school really tight and put another mask over. I was the only one that was able to go in there and rummage through his stuff and just grab as much as I could—for my daughter, mainly, there's nothing that I really needed. I didn't want her to be at the scene. There was blood on the floor. It was just a lot."

In the midst of this shock, she tried to take her licensing exam but didn't pass.

Still, she is determined to try again. She's had more than one experience she believes are signs that this is her calling. She was visiting a friend who worked at a rehab center. And when a resident overdosed during the visit, Masako was able to help perform CPR and save the individual's life. In another incident, Masako witnessed a motorcycle accident. The motorcyclist didn't want to seek medical treatment—he said he had no health insurance. But Masako could see the extent of his injuries and she was able to step in, help him, and convince him to seek additional medical attention. "Everyone else was just standing there staring, in shock," she says. Her ability to step up when needed tells her she's on the right path.

She's planning to reschedule her board exams so that she can accomplish her goal of becoming a registered nurse and finding financial security for herself and her daughter.

"There's so many times where I think about how I went through all this stuff. I went through the nursing program; I went through delays; I grad-uated much later than I anticipated. And I'm not going to say that my ex-husband's death was a delay. I hate to make it lesser than it is—it was a big deal. I needed to pause my life for that. This is giving me time to reflect on our relationship, on the way I feel about all this now. And yes, he was the abuser, and then we had this coparenting relationship that came out of it that was really good. And my daughter and I talk about these things a lot," she says.

"I tend to have the mantra *Just keep moving forward.* So oftentimes, I forget what happened because it's kind of buried behind me." Pushing forward got Masako through a lot of turbulent, difficult times. But right now, that's different. "I made a decision to say, *I'm going to work through this. I'm going to untangle this awful web of yarn or whatever that's inside of me and just try to give myself a break, stop being so hard on myself, stop blaming myself for everything.* I just wanted to really go back and get through some of that stuff so that I could move forward in my life and feel better and not feel bad or not feel shameful or guilty for just doing normal things. There was a lot of stuff that happened, and I'm trying to unravel that."

Today, Masako is continuing to find her way through the process of awakening from her experience. "My story is definitely 'to be continued...,'" she says.

Masako's lesson is this: Sometimes life demands a pause. And though it may seem counterintuitive and contrary to the hustle culture, that pause is essential to progress.

Wisdom from Experience

Jeanna's Story

FOR JEANNA, higher education wasn't just a personal goal. From her vantage point, a degree or even two was an economic necessity.

"I've always been very academic and very educationally driven, so not having a bachelor's degree really wasn't an option. But around here, if you want to get paid more than minimum wage, you need one. And if you want to get paid a livable wage, you need a master's degree," she says.

Jeanna could see the job market around her. Employers who paid well enough to secure an apartment and have a positive future demanded top levels of education. "Even if you have a lot of experience, you still need a master's degree."

The road to that education was long and difficult. As a single mother trying to extricate herself from an abusive relationship and raise a child with emotional and behavioral challenges, staying in school was hard. But Jeanna did the math, and that's what inspired her plan for the future.

"I was twenty-seven and I did some calculations: *I've got probably forty more years of working. Either I do that at a lower rate, or I do it at a higher rate and get my master's now.* So I really prayed about it, really sought the Lord about it, because it's a huge undertaking." At the same time, her relationship with her son's father had only gotten worse. He would not be a source of support, she knew. "It was going to be difficult, but I was in church one day and just asking God to make it clear. And I can't even remember what it was, but it was so clear. And I thought, *Okay, then we're doing this.*"

Jeanna credits WISP for providing key support that enabled her to get where she is today. During her undergraduate education, she had exhausted the Pell Grant and likely would not have qualified for private loans. WISP came through with the assistance to cover the tuition bill. "It was something like twenty-two hundred dollars standing in the way," Jeanna recalls. "I wouldn't have been able to graduate without that.

"Some of the scholarships are very rigid, and rigid does not mix well with day-to-day life. To be able to spend [scholarship] money on things that I needed, like rent or electricity or things like that, was so amazing. And I didn't have to wait for the school to reimburse because that was, again, so prohibitive to be waiting on a couple thousand dollars. Knowing that's coming doesn't pay the bills. So WISP was truly so integral to all of this. I truly don't know if I would be here, sitting in my office making a hundred and thirty-five dollars an hour."

WISP came through with crucial support another time when Jeanna realized she needed to leave a job where a supervisor was abusive. She reached out to WISP for extra help, despite not being sure that the organization would understand. "It was so cathartic to list everything that happened with my supervisor and be believed," she says. "They ended up giving me more money and saying, *We are so proud of you for not staying in such a situation like that.* I remember crying—and I was not a crier then. But I remember just crying for how thankful I was that God provided for me through that."

It was WISP's unique understanding of abusive situations that made the difference, Jeanna recalls. "They understood where I was coming from and were supportive." Other advisors, even her pastor, had encouraged Jeanna to stay in her job, despite the toxic supervisor, until she found a new one. WISP provided Jeanna with the option to leave.

Even with support from WISP, Jeanna faced daunting obstacles.

She was still enduring abuse during her time as an undergraduate student. One assault from her child's father forced her to withdraw from her classes. "But instead of it being a W on my transcript, it was an F. It wrecked my GPA. And I was devastated because I worked so hard. And so, I had to do an appeal. And I had gotten probably close to a hundred pages of documents with the police reports, the court documents, a letter from my therapist, and a letter from me, just begging for mercy, essentially, that they would change it. And they did." Her self-advocacy paid off and she was able to graduate with the accolades she'd earned.

Being present for her son was its own full-time job. "For the first eleven or twelve years of his life, my son has always known Mom to be in school full time, sometimes working full time, sometimes working part time. I'd get up, get him to school, go to work, get him, get him to practice. And then when he was at practice, I'd do my schoolwork, then we'd have dinner, he would do homework, then he'd go to bed. And then I'd have schoolwork till one, two, three in the morning and get up the next day and do it all over again," she says. "I can't tell you how much I don't miss that." Her son's emotional and behavioral needs plunged them both into the complexities of the medical system, further taxing her reserves.

Upon completing her bachelor's in criminal justice, she sought out a master's in social work program, having learned that, as a licensed social worker, she would have lots of job opportunities. Her stellar academic record qualified her to join a prestigious honor society—Alpha Epsilon Lambda—and in the process, she found herself up against another hurdle for women like her. There was a condition that members needed to complete a certain number of volunteer hours, which was an impossibility. "I emailed them and said, *I don't think you mean to be disenfranchising, but here's a brief part of my story, and I can't do those things because I'm too busy raising a child and trying to change systems.*" The organization agreed that their expectations were unrealistic and accepted her into its ranks. "I was really happy about that. That was exciting."

When applying for a job, she was dismayed when funding was cut and the job opportunity was eliminated. But then the hiring manager suggested another option—to open her own business. That's when Jeanna founded her own private practice as a forensic social worker. She works with clients who have open court cases, and she's built her caseload to the point where she sometimes has to turn away business. "I've been doing this full time for over three years. And it's flown by. I've never been in a job this long before, never mind had one that I've liked," she says.

Part of her satisfaction comes from being able to help clients in the way she wishes her abuser could have been helped.

"I just think about his own humanity because I know he had trauma, and I did too, but we just addressed it in different ways. And I had more privileges with my mom than what he ever did with either of his parents. So I think that was a big part of it as well. Not out of pity or excusing him for his behavior, but it's been cathartic to help people who are not entirely guilty. They're not entirely innocent, but they're not entirely guilty, and they're doing the best they can, for the most part."

Being her own boss has been a personal and professional growth experience. "When I've worked for other people, I would have a lot of anxiety. I'd think, *Oh my gosh, I need to do enough, be enough, whatever.* But I really have come into my own in this job, and I learned to be confident in myself and who I am and the work that I am doing. I would not have gotten this working for an agency."

Her success has brought her job offers from agencies, but Jeanna has turned them down. Her private practice provides the financial means and the flexibility to manage her family responsibilities. "I had just turned nineteen when I had my son. I really think that God taught me that I can always get a new job, but he can't get another mom. I've tried to honor that throughout his young life as best as I could, while still trying to pay bills."

She relishes the ability to be effective for her clients—in a way she often did not receive when she herself was in crisis. In her work, Jeanna has become a fierce advocate for those the system may be ready to give up on. She is pushing back on a huge and complex system that can be very unjust. And she frequently draws on her own experience for motivation.

"Nothing has prepared me to do my job better than my personal experience. Because I know what it is like to be so disenfranchised and beat down by systems and policies and procedures that make sense on paper. But when you're living it, it's devastating, and it wrecks your entire life and the lives of the ones that you love the most. I think that is probably why I am so highly sought after—because of my experiences."

There are times she is frustrated by the efforts she makes for her clients, juxtaposed with the lack of effort she perceived the system exerted on her behalf when she was in crisis. She talks, for example, of helping a man who was jailed for violating a restraining order—and his alleged action was tossing an empty bottle on the lawn of his ex as he walked by her home. "Whereas my son's dad strangled me and literally nothing happened to him," she recalls. "That was really hard to deal with."

But she draws great satisfaction from pushing back against a system that can be so oppressive to some, and she often goes above and beyond to help her clients. She traveled to a neighboring state to help a client who'd been extradited. She went the extra mile to help a gang member change his life and have access to programs and education that will help him stay out of jail. She even found a way to offer grace to her abuser at his sentencing hearing. She is happy to see that he has now sought psychiatric help and is doing better on medication. "That's been extremely validating because I would tell providers and judges and DCF Child Protective Services— anybody who would listen—that he had significant mental health issues, that the domestic violence is real. It's not just with me, it's a problem that you need to address."

Jeanna has a firm belief that faith played a role in every one of her experiences. "Jesus has been the answer for me. I think I've been given opportunities and things like that that require a level of obedience and require a level of faith." It's that obedience and faith that have truly landed her in this place where she can be of service to others.

"People will come in here [my office] and they will share things that they don't share with anybody else. I am so honored to be in that place. I'm so privileged to be a keeper of people's deepest feelings."

In that role, Jeanna strives to teach people that other people can be safe. That people do want to help, and that "sharing your whole heart is okay. You're not wrong or bad or crazy. You're just human," she says. "And I can be human too."

Courage to Change Course

Kristen's Story

ONE OF THE THINGS Kristen relishes now is her housing situation.

She lives with her children in a development that is a far cry from her younger days. "I live in a house in a subdivision that has a homeowner's association. I've never lived in anything like it before. We have a community park. We have a community pool. And now my backyard is so big and it's enclosed. I can put a swing set out there for my children and a trampoline and have a spot for my garden."

It is a life wildly different from the patterns laid down by her family for generations. And one that reminds her that her life could have taken a very different turn. "I'm not supposed to be here today. If my life continued to go the way that it was going, I would probably be either serving a life sentence in jail, or I would be dead already."

Getting to her safer, healthier place has been a journey with many helpers along the way. Kristen credits WISP and the local domestic violence shelter, as well as other advisors, who helped her choose the path that was meant for her.

The concrete support and advice of WISP played a critical role in Kristen's decision to take her life in a new direction.

"I was at a fork in the road. One way was clear, and one was hidden. The clear one was the way I've always been living, and generations before me, but I was tired of it. It was not what I wanted. WISP cleared the way for

me to try a new path," she says. "Everyone always says, *Stay in your lane,
stay in your lane.* I don't fit in any of these lanes, so I got to make my own,"
she says. "The WISP scholarship was like a bulldozer to show me that
there was nothing blocking the other path."

Her scholarship paid off her massage therapy program. The balance due
was threatening her ability to complete her education. And perhaps one of
the most important ways WISP helped was to point out a way her abusive
domestic partner was using a financial asset to continue controlling her.

"When I read my own email telling me that I was approved for the
scholarship, it was right there: *Get a new-to-you car. Do not repair the car
that is in your ex's name that is registered to your ex.*" Kristen was amazed that
someone understood the reality of her situation. It was a moment in her
life when she felt truly and accurately seen. "They understood it wasn't just
about me being mobile again. It was about me being mobile and having
the freedom to do what I needed to do for myself and my children. And
as long as I had a car that was in my ex's name, he had power over me.
He could say, *Oh, don't make me come take the car!* Or, *No, I'm not going to
register it.*" About the support she received from WISP, Kristen says, "That
freed me. From that point, I knew I don't have to deal with less than what
I give to others. This was the first car I've ever had in my own name and
I still have it today."

The vehicle was a tangible tie to her abuser—but, even when it was cut,
the emotional abuse continued. "One minute he's trying to love bomb me.
And when he realizes the love bombing ain't working, then he wants to
try to belittle me and put me down. And when that ain't working, now he
wants to be quiet, but he don't realize when he gets quiet, I'm thinking,
Thank you, God!"

Although it's been five years and she's still dealing with the aftermath
of leaving her abuser, things are different now for Kristen. "Getting the
scholarship was a level of kindness I've never experienced before. I was
on the verge of being cold hearted, going against my own caring nature,
changing my outlook on people. My mustard-seed faith in people was
almost gone," she says.

The help she received from WISP allowed her to direct her energies toward her goal of starting a business. "My real goal, the real purpose of my business, is self-care. Because especially as women and mothers and single mothers, we feel like we don't deserve to spend any time on ourselves, any energy on ourselves, any money on ourselves." That can lead women to feel overwhelmed and even depressed, she notes.

And Kristen knows that if she's going to be successful in the business of self-care, she has to start with herself. This realization marked an emotional and spiritual break with her life as a victim of abuse—a role she traces to many years before her entanglement with an abusive partner.

"My family is manipulative and emotionally abusive, and as a result, I attempted to cling to anyone who seemed to genuinely care, ignoring their interactions and relationships with others. I ignored the fact that they display the same behaviors I was running from in my family," she says. "After constantly being put down, made to feel like I was not capable of doing anything worth being proud of, and the attempts to break my spirit, I realized that relationship was not healthy for me or my children," she says.

Her journey forward from that decision has been one of both concrete and sacred steps. She went back to school and studied massage therapy. She secured her salon license. She has worked doing hair and personal care services in her own business and as an employee. She worked to create more financial stability in her own life and more emotional stability for her children.

At the same time, she followed a parallel spiritual path. She works with a spiritual advisor. She has consulted a Buddhist monk. She's added Reiki Master and psychic medium to her repertoire. Her spiritual mentor pushed her to be more in touch with her psychic side. "She said, *You are sabotaging yourself and you don't even realize it. Stay where you're at and just start practicing what you're supposed to be doing.* My first real mediumship consultation was with my cousin, about her boyfriend who had died." It was a powerful experience that helped her realize her journey to success and stability would not be a purely physical one. A spiritual transformation would be part of the process.

For Kristen, finding peace is often a matter of looking back in order to move forward.

"My vision is to help people learn that the people who raised us—they didn't mean any harm, but they didn't know any better. They didn't know that they were supposed to heal. They did not know that the things that they experienced were not okay," she says. Tending to generational wounds is part of her spiritual calling. "When you get to a certain level of healing, you begin with the parental relationships. There comes a point where you all pivot—and they are no longer the parent, they're no longer the teacher. Now you are."

She's writing a book about the topic, titled *Healing Her Mother's Wounds*. "It's talking about generations. And I don't like saying 'generational curses,' because I don't think it's really a curse. I think it's generational ignorance. Because if you don't know, you don't know."

Kristen feels that WISP gave her the backing she needed to face and begin her transformation. "You all just gave me a voice. You all gave me the confidence that I needed to be able to speak out.

"I just really appreciate the fact that I have that peace of mind to be able to go against the grain and not be normal," she says. Defying expectations is what Kristen does. In sharing her story, she gives others the courage to change course—radically if necessary—and follow their own north star.

Looks Can Be Deceiving

Alicia's Story

WHAT DOES SOMEONE WHO needs help look like?

Does she drive a Mercedes?

Is her daughter in private school?

Does she have a job?

You might think that person doesn't look like she needs support. But not everything is as it appears. As Alicia will tell you, "We don't always look like what we've been through."

In her marriage, Alicia knew the violence she was experiencing was not okay. She knew that being choked, getting knocked in the head, and enduring the lying, emotional manipulation, and infidelity was not right. But disengaging was also traumatic.

"What is grief and loss? It's loss of a lifestyle. It's loss of a person. Because I loved him and I wanted to be with him and it's such a huge thing," she recalls. "Men can really mess your mind up. In that moment, I thought, *Alicia, you're not good enough. Alicia, you weren't a good enough wife.*"

But the day-to-day scramble ultimately became unsustainable.

"I read the Bible, and First Corinthians describes love: *Love is patient, love is kind. Love doesn't keep records of wrongs.* And everything about my marriage was not that. And so that let me know that God was nowhere in that mix. We put ourselves together, and that's why it fell apart."

As she moved to divorce her husband, she juggled daily to try and maintain a sense of normalcy for her child. Her ex was contesting the divorce and refusing to provide financial support for their child, using money and the court to exert power and control. Financial pressures were mounting. "I was pulling up in a Mercedes. My daughter was in private school. Yeah. I do work for the government. I do make good money. But I have the bills from when I was in a marriage. I have a car note from when I was in a marriage. I made these decisions based off of two incomes. And here we are—bam—and he's not helping. My life was just in a mess," she recalls.

Then came the key moment when Alicia knew that something had to give.

"I received a layoff letter. I was working for the county. I was working for the Public Guardian's office. The layoff letter really shocked my soul because I was going through a divorce, and he was withholding finances. And I thought, *What am I going to do?* I started looking for other jobs. Most of the jobs that had higher pay required a master's degree. So I said, *Well, I've got to go get my master's.*"

She chose psychology, inspired in part by her own need to understand why things were happening the way that they were, and also by her own experience in counseling during her divorce. "I really had to seek understanding, and that is what pushed me to choose psychology. I could have picked any major to get a master's." But Alicia saw the impact a good counselor had left on her life and she wanted to help others in the same way.

The plan demanded sacrifice and Alicia was determined to make it work. She left her newly built home to move back with her mother—it was Alicia, her daughter, and their dog all crowded into her old high school bedroom. But even then, Alicia needed financial support to pursue her next step. A counselor told her about WISP. When she read the program's description, she knew this was what she needed to execute her plan.

WISP provided funds for a critical and specific need—childcare in the form of private school tuition. The flexibility of WISP funding which is for "education-related living expenses" allows each recipient to determine how funds are best used according to her unique circumstances. While some might wonder how a child's private school fits this parameter, in Alicia's case, it was a necessary expense. It gave her daughter continuity during a time when the rest of her life was chaos, and it beautifully filled the gaps of before- and after-school care. Even with a WISP scholarship, pursuing a master's degree was not easy, she recalls. She knew she didn't "look the part." And her message is: You don't know what's going on in someone's life.

The demands of a master's program can be especially taxing on a single mother, says Alicia. "I had to move back home with my mom because of finances. Also, I needed to do an internship. The internship was unpaid, and I was trying to graduate, but it was taking so long to get the internship hours. I took a leave of absence from work so I could do the internship full time and quickly graduate. Now I had no pay, but still had to pay my baby's tuition so she could go to school."

Alicia was motivated to seek out what she needed to make that happen. She convinced her professor to tutor her, setting the goal of passing her proficiency exams on the first try. "The professor said, *Sometimes people don't pass the first time.* And I said, *No, I have to pass. Me and my daughter are living in my high school bedroom with the dog. I want my own place, and I just want to be able to go back to work and get a better job and start our new normal.* She said, *Okay.* And she tutored me once a week on Tuesdays during her lunch break."

And Alicia achieved her goal, passing her exam on her first try.

Now, nearly fifteen years out, she can reflect on the results.

"I can only imagine, oh Lord, what my life would be if I wasn't able to obtain my master's degree, get a job that was higher paying, which allowed me to not have to go back. That's the main thing, to not have to go back. A lot of women go back to those domestically violent situations because they can't do it on their own. They stick and stay in situations because they're not able to maintain or to live that lifestyle. They put up and shut up."

Alicia realized having her additional education was the critical factor that allowed her to be able to support herself and her daughter in the way she saw fit. "I would not have been able to do it without WISP giving me the scholarship. It allowed me to get my master's, which allowed me to get a better job, which allowed me to increase my income. It was the one thing that started building on everything else," she says. "Sometimes a giver doesn't realize the magnitude of the gift—a gift that keeps on giving."

Her improved financial status allowed Alicia to make broader long-term plans regarding the life she wanted for herself and for her daughter.

"After I graduated and I was still at my mom's, I hired a realtor because I needed to find a place. The realtor asked, *So what are you looking for?* And I said, *A good school district.* He said, *No, I'm talking about how many bedrooms, etc.* I told him, *I can make any house a home. Put me in a good school district."* Education continued to be top priority for Alicia.

Today, Alicia has made the life she wanted. Her education was what allowed her to increase her earnings and return to the lifestyle she had when married, but this time on her own. Now remarried, she became the educated, successful, classy woman she reaches out to through her Spoiled Wives Club.

"I'm here at this juncture of happiness, and it was mind-boggling to me as to why people, even individuals that knew what I've been through, weren't able to celebrate with me. You know how sometimes people can be happy for you? They want you to be happy, but not happier than them? They want me to have a man, but not a better man than theirs. The good stuff they want to minimize. They only want a little of it. They want to hear the drama. It was very disappointing. And that's what made me create the Spoiled Wives Club community because I want to be around other women who are loved this way. Their husbands love them. They're happy to be married. And it's not a problem if you're happy about something that happened in your marriage. What is wrong with that? There's nothing wrong with that. There's nothing wrong with being loved this way. And many people, if they dig deep, they want to be loved this way."

"Spoiled" may not fit with the preconceived notion some hold about what recipients of financial help should want. Breaking that conception is part of Alicia's goal. Spoiled, according to Alicia, means being treated with the respect and loyalty you deserve. It is believing in your own self-worth and allowing love to be demonstrated in concrete ways—yes, maybe even a Mercedes.

Other people's perceptions are not her problem, says Alicia. Any criticisms others have are "something that they have to conquer—the Negative Committee that meets in their mind."

Alicia is also moving forward to expand her professional goals. She's working on her memoir, she's working as a counselor, utilizing her advanced degree. She's started a podcast with her husband called *The Family Dynamics*, to explore topics of marriage and blended families. She's ventured into the entrepreneurial realm as a wedding and event planner.

Her daughter is in college now, with big dreams of her own—entering from her top-performing high school with a slew of advanced credits.

And Alicia has started a scholarship in her mother's memory. Her mother, Donna Burton, who passed away in 2019, had been a longtime employee of Hillcrest High School outside of Chicago, Illinois. The scholarship honors her mother's service to the school.

Alicia continues to be open about her experiences—the good and the bad. "When you're going through the domestic violence, it seems as if everybody else's marriage is perfect. Everybody else's husband is perfect. You're the only one with this crazy person. You're the only one with this dysfunctional marriage." She shares her story so others will know they aren't alone.

And she continues to tell the world at large: Check your assumptions. Examine them. And deal with them.

Leading with Love

Kinna's Story

KINNA IS SURE HER LIFE—and her pain—has a purpose.

"I've been through quite a bit. I've survived six rapes. I've survived child molestation and incest. I survived being sex trafficked three times. I started using drugs when I was twelve to cope. That was the age I first attempted suicide. By the time I was fifteen, I had started using IV drugs." Kinna endured so many traumas that it would be difficult to put them all in one story. Still, she shares it all so that others will know that there is hope. "I don't think that I went through all of this just to sit and do nothing with my life. I want women to know that you can make it. Your past doesn't have to predict your future."

She credits her faith in God for helping her to survive and achieve a stable, successful life. But she acknowledges that even faith can be a challenging road. At first, believing that she could be loved and forgiven just filled her mind with more questions.

"I was still wondering, *Why would You let all this happen to me?* I was still angry. It took me reading more and watching more lessons and sermons to understand I was chosen. Those things that happened to me made me who I am. He already knew that I was stubborn. I see it from a different perspective now. I feel special that God even chose me because a lot of people don't get chosen. A lot of people don't make it out the street. A lot of the people that I was out there with, they're dead or really sick. And it's just sad. But I trust God." She holds to her faith that God would not have brought her this far just to let her fall. That realization was a turning point in her mind.

Kinna's educational path involved a string of unexpected hurdles. She left school when she left home at age twelve. Later, she was able to get her GED. She was living in a shelter when the topic of school came up during a goal-planning session with her advocate. She started taking college courses and acing them, earning spots on the dean's list and president's list, and was inducted into Phi Theta Kappa. She realized she was smart—despite so many in her past telling her otherwise.

Just as she was poised to start her bachelor's degree, family needs pulled her out of school again. But eventually, she returned to college, eager to continue her studies in psychology. In many ways, the coursework was part of her personal journey—she wanted not just to master the material, but to understand herself and how events in her life had shaped her. She graduated with a dual degree in psychology and sociology.

WISP was part of her educational support system, both financially and emotionally. "There's no way I would have got this far without you guys," Kinna affirms. For one thing, it was the cost—paying for tuition was out of reach. She also recalls the little ways WISP showed support, like the weekly Motivational Monday Messages that WISP emails to all current and former participants. "It was encouraging," she says. "I still read them all the time." She realized that emotional support was as valuable as financial support in her educational undertaking, "especially after coming from what I've been through."

Inspired by the encouragement she received from her advocate at the domestic violence shelter, Kinna works to help others like herself—women who experienced domestic violence who do not have children. This is a gap in the domestic violence–response ecosystem that she has personally experienced.

She founded Kinna's House of Love to address that gap, and while she has not yet raised the funds to buy a building, she is already providing support to this underserved community by collecting and distributing things like winter coats and school supplies and hosting events such as a tea party and a disco-dancing ball.

She's also founded Kinna's Corner, a space for kids who are working through trauma. She began the project in memory of a young child in her community who was murdered.

"The anger I have from not enjoying my childhood, I apply that now, even in my adulthood. And I think some adults need to do this. Don't be mad because you didn't get to have fun when you were a kid. You can have fun now," she says. And she walks that talk when she throws an event for children—a tea party, a bubble show, a dance event—she's having just as much fun as they are.

Kinna meets needs with action. She's usually the first to jump in and is good at rallying others to her cause. "Everything I started, I actually started from my home. I had a clothing closet on my porch. I take food down to the shelter on Sundays. I cook for sixty or more people. I do it by myself most of the time. The pleasure I get is that I pray with them, and they look forward to that more than they do anything."

And that's not all. She formed a group, drawing from the school board and local agencies, to go into schools to talk to young students about domestic violence. It's important, she says, to start this kind of education early.

There are times when Kinna feels like her work is to make direct connections within the community one person at a time. According to her faith, it's not about her, it's about serving other people. "I hug people a lot. I'm a hugger. One time I was doing a Christmas meal, and one of the guys who always calls me 'Sis' is there. He's a tall white dude. He was missing his family, and I gave him a hug. He just broke down right there."

Often she will draw on her own experiences to give advice to others, such as the process for applying to have a criminal record expunged. She helped organize an expungement event, in which lawyers volunteered to participate and advise attendees. Kinna can understand how much of an impact expungement can have. "People will be more motivated to want to do better." Otherwise, they may not make the effort to pursue a job or education, assuming the criminal record will lead to a rejection. "They ain't going to hire me. I'm not even going to try."

Kinna is an advocate not just at the grassroots level but as a force for broader change. She encourages others to advocate for change that will help a community.

"The system is unforgiving. It's not that people don't want to change. It's the system that won't let you," she says. She hears complaints about "the system" all the time, but few seem to want to make the effort necessary to achieve change. "Everybody's complaining about the system, but there's nobody messing with the system. Why don't you all help us? If you all want a better community, why not help us?" She challenges complacency with questions and is unafraid to take on challenges, ready to call her state representative or even the president if the situation requires it.

She's been recognized for her efforts. Although her natural inclination is to steer clear of the spotlight, she accepts the recognition in order to further her mission. She is often sought out for interviews on local news stations, and she represented Iowa at the Remarkable Woman Award ceremony in Los Angeles. She was honored with a Hometown Hero Award for her work with single, unhoused women. And she received the Pay It Forward Award for providing home-cooked meals to unhoused people in her community. She recently traveled to New York City as a nominee for the National Jefferson Awards—a prestigious award that honors public service. Past recipients include Oprah Winfrey, former president Jimmy Carter, and Shaquille O'Neal.

Her faith remains her cornerstone. "Some days I don't even know which way to go. I pray and I ask God. It's stressful allowing God to lead you versus planning things yourself. But I don't want to mess it up, so I try to do my best to let God guide me in whatever I do."

Kinna wears a sweatshirt that she designed, printed with the words from First Corinthians chapter sixteen, verse fourteen: "Let all things you do be done in love." Love is the foundation of her every action, and she has a special way of knowing what others need because of her own past experiences. When she reaches out in love to tend to someone else's pain, in some small way she's also tending to her own. Because what goes around, comes around. Especially love.

Shaping a Movement

Kalyn's Story

KALYN HAD A "GOOD" JOB in human resources for a health-care company when she realized she could do better.

She had a position that put her in contact with the C-suite, with the vice presidents, with the owner. And then one day while she was working on payroll in her office, she saw it: Some of her colleagues made as much as three times her salary. "And I'm thinking, *They're not three times as smart as I am. I'm actually smarter than some of them. The only reason why they're getting paid more than me is because they have a degree, and I don't.*"

It was this realization that galvanized Kalyn to seek higher education. Supported by a WISP scholarship, she was able to complete a bachelor's and a master's. With those degrees, she went on to achieve two important life goals: to be paid what she was worth and be a leader in the fight against domestic violence. "I wanted not just to be a part of the movement, but to shape the movement," she says.

But it was a difficult journey to that position of achievement.

Kalyn still feels the physical impact of her abuser who, among other injuries, shattered her eye socket and left her with residual damage. "My mother had to actually give them a photo of what I looked like so they could put everything back together," she recalls. In addition to the physical abuse, Kalyn's abuser made it impossible for her to finish college, even though she had a scholarship to pursue her degree in fine arts. But as a now single mother, in the process of disentangling from an abusive relationship,

Kalyn was determined to be successful. "I have to have this for my kids. I could have given up on myself, but I wasn't giving up on them."

After her "a-ha!" moment preparing the company payroll, Kalyn immediately turned to the task of finding funding to restart her educational career. That very day. "At lunch, I decided to search for a scholarship. I said, *You know what? I'm Black, I'm older, I'm a woman, I have all these different things that I should be able to qualify for some kind of scholarship.* I started to look through this database, and it literally took me my whole lunch.

"It was one of those complicated databases that wanted all your information. So I'm scrolling through the results, scrolling through, scrolling through. I get to the last page. I was about to close it and just give up. And I said, *Well, I'm already at the last page. Let me just look at this last one.* I clicked on it. It was the Sunshine Lady Foundation. And I said, *I'm a survivor! Destiny!*"

She called her mom, and together they put hours into the application. At the time, Kalyn didn't meet certain eligibility criteria, but she was determined. "I felt like if I stated a strong enough reason why I should get it anyway because of what I went through, it was no way I could have returned [to school] earlier than that." And WISP agreed.

When she talks about her experience with WISP, Kalyn says, "I talk so highly about the program and I'm like, the program is still supporting me and my family. My daughter is a recipient now and she's about to actually go on a study abroad to Germany. I'm just so blessed. And being connected with WISP has been such a blessing to me on so many levels. I mean, from being able to talk to you to other support that was given has been helpful so many times through the years. It has really made the difference between, honestly, life or death for me and my family, financially and just all of it."

Even with financial and emotional support from WISP, Kalyn found the higher education process challenging. So many elements from other aspects of her life emerged as hurdles. She was laid off from her corporate job. She struggled to launch an independent consulting business. Her responsibilities—including her recently purchased home—piled high.

But in her heart, she knew she was meant to create an entrepreneurial venture. And the inspiration came in part from an experience she'd had during her years in HR. She was writing a woman up for low productivity. She had the employee in her office and was giving her a verbal warning when the woman suddenly started to tell Kalyn about abuse she was suffering at home. The woman said to Kalyn, *I know this would never happen to you.* Kalyn was stunned.

"She finishes, and I said, *Girl, why you think it would never happen to me? Yeah, I've been there,*" she says. "We talked about some strategies and some things I could help her with in HR moving forward. And when she left out the office, I leaned back into my chair and I thought, *Why would she think that this could happen to her, but it couldn't happen to me? Is it because I don't look like I have injuries, thank God? Because I work in the C-suite? Because I wear a suit every day?*"

Kalyn realized her background in business and human resources gave her a unique way to reach women who were in abusive situations. She went home from work that day and began to sketch the entrepreneurial idea that was forming in her mind.

"I was sitting on the edge of the bed and had a pad of paper. I was kind of in a trance, as if God was writing this and my hands were just moving on their own. SAFE, SAFE, SAFE. Sisters Acquiring Financial Empowerment. I could see it: *You're going to have ladies' tea, and you're going to do economic work and help with job searching and resume writing and budgeting.*"

Later, when her first attempts to start a consulting business faltered, she decided this was a sign that she had started the wrong business. The business she was supposed to start was SAFE.

"I started SAFE right when I was about to graduate with my bachelor's degree," she says. And it was a lot of balls to juggle. "I'm starting a new business. I'm in school. I'm a single mom, with a house, a family. And I'm trying to provide direct services and be out there marketing and promoting this work."

But while SAFE was successful, running it proved a challenge for Kalyn. She found her family responsibilities suffered. "I felt like the cobbler whose kids have no shoes," she says. Kalyn struggled financially for years. Essentially, she was living two lives—one was a very successful and dynamic leader in the nonprofit world, and the other was a woman scraping pennies together to pay her mortgage.

Thanks to her work in founding and running SAFE, she was invited to meet the then vice president Joe Biden. And she did, but she could barely afford it and had to couch surf while she was in Washington, DC, because paying for a hotel was out of the question. She was teaching financial empowerment to others but financially struggling herself. SAFE provided excellent services to the community but never paid her a salary. The mortgage was always in jeopardy, she recalls. The kids needed things.

In one of her scholarship renewal applications for WISP, Kalyn wrote about her desire to start a nonprofit organization. "And I feel really proud that I did. And not only did I do it, but I rocked that thing. The fact that the White House called me about my work and that they featured it, that's crazy. One Black girl from Detroit making moves, helping survivors. Even today, so many people tell me, *Because of your organization, I'm in a better place. My kids are doing better.*"

She was dedicated to serving survivors through SAFE, but ultimately the responsibilities of work and family became unsustainable. "It means a lot that I ran SAFE until 2013. In 2009 I started to really get burnt out from vicarious trauma, but I kept the momentum going super high. And then, because the demand was there, I was doing consulting. I'm doing all these different things because SAFE never paid me." It was a period of high personal stress.

Also in 2013, Kalyn suffered a huge personal loss when her mother died unexpectedly. It was the catalyst for a major life shift. "It was such a blow. It was like everything just stopped, and I just felt lost," she says. It was a few months later when a friend suggested she break away from the deep grief and go on vacation. Somewhat hesitantly, Kalyn agreed. It was on that vacation in St. Thomas that she met the man she would marry a year and a half later. And then, ultimately made the move to St. Thomas herself. During this time, she shifted her skills and focus in another direction. She turned over the management of SAFE to a new director and moved into staff positions for domestic violence groups. First with the Institute on Domestic Violence in the African American Community, then with the Virgin Islands Domestic Violence and Sexual Assault Council, and currently with Ujima, Inc.: The National Center on Violence Against Women in the Black Community. She found she was able to give support and guidance to the movement within this new context while being compensated in a way that matched her value, even receiving a tremendous amount of support in difficult personal times, such as when she underwent treatment for stage 2 breast cancer.

This ability to choose where to live and work in the domestic violence prevention field at jobs that suited her individual needs is something she knows is a direct outcome of her educational experience. Her education fully validated her value and her power. "At the end of the day, I have two degrees under my belt and experience. I can land on my feet. I can make it happen. Having my degrees really empowered me to make personal decisions as well as professional decisions," she says. "My education has been so liberating and empowering for me. I can say, *I have my degrees. I'm qualified for this job. I'm qualified to speak at this place.* That made a difference for me on so many levels, for me to say I am an expert and an authority."

Reflecting on her experience, Kalyn says she can see the impact her education had on her own life, the lives of her children, and even the larger trajectory of her family.

"We were eating dinner the other night, and my youngest daughter asked, *Am I the first person who's going to actually graduate from college straight from high school?* I said, *Yes*." This breaks a generational cycle for the family, Kalyn says. And WISP is still there for support—her daughter is attending school with a scholarship for children of WISP graduates.

Kalyn's story is a reminder to all of us that every piece in the process makes a difference, and to keep stepping out in faith.

All Is Not Lost

Daria's Story

LIFE CAN TAKE UNEXPECTED DETOURS. But you can still get to where you're going.

That's Daria's message. She knows firsthand how far off track an unfortunate choice in domestic partners can take you. But, she says, "Where I have landed has a lot to do with where I started before everything went sideways."

Her first partner physically abused her. When she became pregnant, Daria's father gave her a choice: give up her child and he'd keep paying for school. It was a deal she was unwilling to make, so she had to drop out of college. She eventually made the decision to leave her first partner, but that still left her without a clear way to support herself and her child.

"When I was twenty-one, I got pregnant by a man who picked me up and tossed me by my neck. So I cut that off and that was smart. But then I was a single mother at twenty-one years old. I had started dating the man who would later become my husband, and he was fine. For a while."

As a young, single mom, Daria's natural affinity for technology seemed a promising way to improve her economic situation.

"I learned how to program in BASIC when I was nine. I was very comfortable with computers in a way that most people weren't at that point in time. I went after an IT career, full tilt. I initially got a job as a receptionist for a tech support company and worked my way into a tech support position. And then from the tech support position, I went to Sprint as an IT consultant."

All that painted a rosy picture for Daria's future—but her choice of partners came back to haunt her. Daria now earned twice what her husband was making—an imbalance that infuriated him. "That was when he got mean and stuff started going sideways," she says. He expressed his anger physically, beating her so badly that he broke her neck, requiring surgery to mitigate the damage, leaving scars she still bears to this day. She bore the full responsibility for the household. And he launched a psychological warfare campaign, interfering with her sleep—so severely that it impaired her ability to function normally and impacted her job performance.

"I was trying to be a full-time IT consultant for some pretty high-end clients—the DOJ, the Federal Reserve," she says. "This was a high-profile, big-demand job and I was not getting enough sleep to do it. And it broke me. It just broke me and it broke the career."

When layoffs came at Sprint, Daria was one of the first to go. Her checkered job performance made her an easy target. The loss of her job plunged the family into a desperate financial situation.

"From that point forward, we lived in grinding, ridiculous poverty, like food-bank level poverty," she says. "I remember when my son was born, we ran out of oil in the dead of one of the worst winters. It was the winter of 2002–2003, and it was a really bad winter. One time, when our son was an infant, I remember sitting in the middle of the kitchen floor in front of the oven with him in my lap and my daughter next to me in front, just trying to stay warm. That was the life that we lived."

And yet, Daria was convinced at the time that staying with her husband was her only option.

"He had me so spun up in my head and convinced that I couldn't function without him. He made me feel that I was completely incapable of sanity, incapable of anything," she says.

It was when her husband turned his abusive behavior on their son that Daria made the decision to end the relationship. But she decided the safest way out was to make it seem like it was his idea. "It took about a year of quiet, constant pressure to get him to think that he wanted to leave on his own. And he did."

But even then, it was difficult to make a clean break. Daria's abuser was willing to go to great lengths to continue his psychological warfare.

"He started terrorizing me. He moved in directly next door, couch surfing at our neighbor's house. I woke up one morning to the sound of him coughing. And when you're with someone for twenty years, you know that sound. He was directly across the alleyway from my bedroom window on the neighbor's porch roof, having a cigarette." He took aim at their child too. "He would show up at the school to try and take our son out in the middle of the day. He threatened the principal."

Her abuser was tireless, and worse, he seemed to enjoy it. "He was a master, and he loved to manipulate as a sport. That was literally something he was completely open about. *I can manipulate you any way I want to, and you can't do anything about it, even though you know I'm doing it.* He would tell me that. He would tell other people that. And he was good at it. He was a master at terror. He was a master at puppeteering."

What's more, he engaged in an ugly, drawn-out battle for custody.

"We got, literally, according to both the court advocate and my lawyer, the worst judge in the county. And I believe it by how little was done for so long. She let my ex get away with all kinds of things that no other judge would have let him get away with. Unfortunately, my son was stuck in the situation in a fifty-fifty custody arrangement. He was struggling in school, of course, because of the whole situation. And his father's idea of how to get my son to do his homework was to punch the wall next to his face, that kind of stuff. And at one point he actually punched him in the stomach to discipline him. And that was how we finally got him." Daria and her son both called Child Protective Services and eventually the courts awarded them with a Protection from Abuse order.

Even so, Daria had to fight every step of the way to finally get full custody. The conflicts kept Daria's abuser as a constant presence in her life, even as she tried to move on with her new husband.

Her second husband's mother was living with them when Daria's ex tried to break into their house. "She chased him off with a shotgun," Daria recalls. "The very next day was the final custody hearing. He was a no-show. So I got full legal and physical custody." The outcome made it clear: The custody battle was never about their son; it was about using the court to perpetuate the abuse.

It was during the fight for custody that Daria saw her opportunity to change her life and return to the professional status she'd once held. She'd started the degree while still married but had to quit when the jealousy that drove him to undermine her Sprint job emerged again. "He said when I graduated that I would think I was above him or that I wouldn't need him. He tried to sabotage that, but it didn't work. I'm stubborn."

She was ineligible for financial aid because of the length of time she'd been in school and how many classes she had to retake because of interference from her abuser. "A court advocate suggested to me since I didn't have money left to go back to school, that I look for a scholarship. And my brain went *ding, ding, ding.* That's a fantastic idea. And that's how I found WISP." She was out of financial aid but needed less than $7,500 to finish. "I could not have done it on my own. I just ran out of money. WISP was the only way I could have gotten that done. It might have been a million for all I could get. You guys moved that mountain out of my way."

It was a bumpy road. Daria found it necessary to stop and start again more than once. But eventually, she graduated with a bachelor's in accounting.

Now, Daria is poised to start a new job in tech consulting, with a six-figure salary—a job she wouldn't qualify for without her accounting degree plus all of her experience in IT. It will allow her to improve her lifestyle, pay for her son's education, and pursue her favorite activities: dancing, coding, and writing.

She gives back to the community by using her own experiences to reach out to others, one-on-one. "I brought my son's former coworker into our home as a roommate to get her away from her abuser. My son spotted her bruises and behavior instantly," she says. "He came home and asked me to give her a haven. I couldn't turn her away."

Her story is a message to others: You can lose everything and still win.

Severe emotional, physical, and financial abuse takes a toll. Talking about it still causes stress and consternation. It helps that her now husband is incredibly supportive. "He's very patient. He's incredibly encouraging. Every little accomplishment I have he says, *You can do this*. And that's been very healing."

And Daria has tapped enormous reserves of her own emotional grit and resiliency. "It was sheer stubbornness, I guess. A lot of active healing, a lot of therapy, a lot of writing. And the fact that coding was literally my favorite thing. What I did as a consultant before was literally my favorite thing in the world. And having lost that, someone else taking it away from me. That couldn't stand. I didn't want him to win. I wanted me back."

For Daria, the end was also the beginning. "I went to the very bottom, hit the bottom, laid there for a little while. But then I thought, *Okay, I'm not dead. I'm not going to stay here.*"

Daria's story is proof that all is not lost, even when it seems that way.

Breaking the Cycle

Cynthia's Story

CAN YOU BE IN an abusive relationship and not realize it?

Absolutely. From the inside, sometimes the abuse is just not clear.

"I was in denial. Straight up, I was in denial," she recalls. The fact that the abuse escalated to physical violence only a couple of times kept Cynthia from confronting her reality. But all the while, her abuser was causing her harm. "It was more emotional manipulation and mental abuse," she says. Emotional abuse is insidious. It creeps up on you slowly, and that can be tough to see.

Why? One reason is the way current culture socializes women to behave in demure, even submissive ways, she explains. We're told from an early age that we should be people pleasers and that we should put others' needs before our own. We're raised to ignore our own boundaries. It's a mindset that makes you vulnerable to abusive emotional manipulation, she says. "It put me in a place where I would say, *Oh, it's all okay.*"

The cultural conditioning is so pervasive that even those in Cynthia's circle failed to see how difficult it can be to take action to make the abuse stop. "I think what made it worse is that a lot of people around me didn't know what it meant to be in an abusive relationship. They would say, *Oh, somebody's just telling you words. Why don't you block them? Why don't you just stop listening to them?* And I would say, *If it were that easy, I would do it.*"

It took two professionals—a therapist and a domestic violence counselor—to help Cynthia see what was happening. And to understand what to call it.

"My therapist was the one who said, *I think this is what's going on.*" When she referred Cynthia to a domestic violence agency, Cynthia balked, but her therapist pushed forward. "She said, *I'll sit and call with you.* And then from there, the ball got rolling. I had an appointment with an advocate, and she told me it's an abusive relationship. I still think about that moment. If she hadn't said it, I'm not sure if I would have ever recognized it myself. I would have just thought it was just somebody being difficult. I'm just dealing with a difficult person."

But knowing the truth and changing course to follow a new path are two different things. Cynthia struggled to get the help she needed to move away from her abuser.

"The journey was just so long," she says. "At first, I didn't know how the system worked. I didn't have enough data, information, proof, to be able to get a restraining order."

Even as she gained the necessary knowledge to obtain a restraining order, her abuser went to great lengths to evade legal intervention. "He went into incognito mode. I couldn't find him. I didn't know where he was. I didn't know his address. He would hide his car. It was just horrific." As a result, Cynthia couldn't get a restraining order in place because her abuser stayed one step ahead of the process servers. "The restraining order was dragged out because he needed to be served. Where are you going to serve him if you don't have an address?"

What's more, her abuser knew exactly how to stay in her life without getting caught. He would stay away on most arranged visitation days for their son, knowing a server could try to find him there. But he'd turn up in other places, such as their son's first day of school, where a server would not be waiting. Adding to Cynthia's anxiety was the fact that law enforcement officials seemed to be as unsure as she was about how to keep him away. "The police came and took a report, and the officer was asking questions about restraining orders, such as how they work. And I thought, *Oh my God, why do you not know these things? There's a dangerous situation where this man could pop up on me in two seconds and you don't know how a restraining order works?"* The best the police could offer Cynthia was to look around and see if he was in the immediate vicinity.

Cynthia's legal issues dragged on, but that did not stop her from pursuing her education. Cynthia realized that education was the way for her to move on—to find a higher-paying job and a stronger sense of self.

"The gift that I received from WISP was a sense of self-worth," she says. "When I applied for a WISP scholarship, I was in the middle of leaving an unhealthy relationship. It was a very dark time and space in which I was uneasy about my future. As a single mother of two, finances were extremely tight and I had no more outside support. The WISP scholarship that I received twice allowed me to help pay for tuition and receive my diploma."

A friend tipped Cynthia off to the existence of a book listing scholarships. "I got it from the library. My son was still less than a year old, so I had him on my lap while I went through every single page. I looked at the dates, looked at which ones I qualified for. And I saw WISP."

The decision to pursue higher education was a radical one for Cynthia. When she received her bachelor's in sociology, she was the first in her family to do so. "I was the first to get a college degree. And I didn't have enough information about finances, loans, scholarships. Nobody in my family had done this. So I was just going with what I knew, or what I was told, or what my options were. As a woman of color, first of the family to do all of that, yeah, it's a lot." She went beyond her bachelor's, and today Cynthia is the only member of her family to have earned a master's degree.

Even with Pell Grants and scholarships, Cynthia estimates that her undergraduate degree put her at roughly $50,000 in student loan debt. With the master's, she's at $100,000. A staggering number, to be sure, but without help, she figures her student loan debt could have reached upward of $120,000.

As a first-generation college student, Cynthia had to navigate every step of the educational process by herself, without the benefit of family help or role models. It pushed her into conversations she wasn't always eager to have. "It's still taboo to talk about money and scholarships. A lot of people just don't talk about it." That makes education an even greater challenge to a newcomer to the system. But Cynthia knows that without the financial assistance, she might never have achieved her educational success. And for her, the degrees are key to more income, and that's the way she's going to leverage her family out of the cycle of generational poverty. "I didn't just go to school for fun. I didn't just go to school just to get a degree. I see my degrees now and say, *Okay, that's a piece of paper and another piece of paper hanging over there.* But at the same time, it's like those pieces of paper are getting me more money that's going to be able to move my family forward. And even if I don't get to where I want to be while I'm here, at least my kids will know they have options. All the options that I didn't have and was able to pave the way for."

As she studied sociology and worked as an advocate while still managing her own complicated life, Cynthia was better able to recognize the barriers that she and women like her face. Transportation, for example, becomes a major issue if you don't live in a large city with a robust mass transit system. Cynthia had to leave a postgraduate job because the commute from her small city to the big city jobsite was too much of a burden. And when she looked at some government assistance programs, bringing her classroom knowledge and her personal experience together, she wondered if some programs designed to help lower-income people can backfire. She cites the Section 8 housing program, which helps many struggling people, but comes with an income cap. "The mindset is you're on Section Eight and you have to make a certain amount of money so that your bills don't go up, so you can afford the cost of living." Earning more money is, she says, "almost like a punishment."

Cynthia had to change that mindset, and it meant breaking with a way many in her life had been thinking for their whole lives. "But that's the price that I'm going to have to pay to get out of this generational trap that we've been in since I've been growing up. I purposely and willingly continue to look for the information to move myself and my family out of where we've been." She continues, "You can see how people can get stuck into playing small, being small, and not wanting to grow."

Her first job after completing her undergraduate degree was as a court advocate at the same agency where she first learned she was in an abusive relationship. "I was doing advocate work. I used to float between three courts. Honestly, when people hear that they say, *That's so hard to do.* And I say, *That was my favorite job.*"

It was her favorite because it showcased the importance of advocates. "We don't necessarily know how important advocates are. But they are," she says. Cynthia recalls the times she tried and failed to get what she needed from the court system. "I didn't have enough information. I didn't really know what I was doing. I had an advocate, but I don't think they really led me well. But at the end of the day, they were there next to me, standing next to me, sitting in front of the judge, sitting next to me in the courtroom. And that's huge."

To give back to her community, Cynthia has launched an awareness campaign on social media, talking about issues like intimate partner abuse and her own healing journey. It's scary, she says, to put your true self online for everyone to see and comment on, including her abuser.

"At the end of the day, my son's father is still the same. So I'm mindful about what information I put out. He could always circle back into my life because that's what he likes to do. But at the same time, I absolutely cannot let this one person stop me from sharing all of this information with somebody who may need it." She shares her own knowledge and experience to help others who may need to hear about it. "I've had people message me privately on Facebook asking for advice."

And she tells her story so that others may see the patterns in their own lives. She remembers when she had difficulty framing her experience as abuse. "So many people just don't know, and especially when it comes to how you've grown up or what you're used to seeing, people think, *Oh, well, we're just arguing all the time.* Or, *He's just yelling at me, that's just the way he is.* A lot of people don't like to talk about it—or pretend that it's not a thing, but it is." Her truth-telling validates the experiences of others.

Cynthia is a trailblazer. Whether it's breaking the taboo of silence that surrounds domestic violence, discussing finances, or breaking out of generational patterns. And she's determined to take others with her by sharing the information she worked so hard to get. "It's just going to be a forever passion to let people know that there's options out there."

Clarity in an Instant

Amy's Story

THERE WERE TIMES DURING the worst of Amy's abuse when she wondered if it would be better if her husband hit her. Then, at least people would believe her.

Amy lived seventeen years in a marriage where abuse was intense and routine, but she told no one outside the family. And no one outside the family could see it.

The verbal and emotional abuse was baked into her daily life. Her husband raged if the dinner was not cooked to his specifications. He raged at the children if the TV remote was not right by his chair when he got home from work. Amy scrambled constantly to keep him happy by trying to anticipate his needs, no matter how outrageous. "When you're living in it, you just keep adjusting to whatever the new crazy is," she recalls.

When she one day worked up the courage to stand up for her children and confront her husband about his behavior, she was stunned at his response.

"He literally said, *Oh, it was never about the TV. I just have all the stress at work and this is my only release.* That was actually worse, because in my head, I always figured if he just understood the impact of his actions, he wouldn't do it. So that was a big, powerful moment. *He actually totally knows what he's doing. He just thinks it's okay.*"

The stress from living with his episodes of rage was so intense that Amy suffered from tremors that affected her ability to walk. She was diagnosed with MS. It wasn't until after she left her husband that the truth about her symptoms emerged.

Amy's breaking point came when her husband threatened to kill her daughter's dog.

"He told our oldest, who was fourteen, that she had to get rid of her dog by the end of the week or he'd get rid of it for her." Amy knew that in her rural town, that was code for a bullet. "My oldest had basically protected this dog from her dad for six months. And now he was going to go shoot it if we didn't find a place."

When she could not find another home, Amy's daughter put all her concerns and objections into a letter to her father. "I saw it, and I thought, *He is going to be so furious.* But I couldn't censor her because what she wrote was true. She was writing about how she felt with the events of that weekend and then all the things over the years, stuff I hadn't even really remembered, because you can only hold so much anger before it just kind of leaks out."

Predictably, Amy's husband exploded when confronted with his daughter's letter. "He saw it and he started screaming. The kids were right upstairs, they could hear everything. He told me I could crumple the letter up and shove it up her ass, that she was an ungrateful little bitch who'd had everything handed to her on a silver platter. I just had this absolute clarity. I'd wanted to leave for years, but I kept thinking I had to stay and fix the finances before I could leave. I just had this clarity: *I can't be here,*" she says.

"The last epiphany I had in leaving, literally, was that I was figuring out what my choices really were. Because I wanted so badly to be in a home with my kids, in a happy marriage. That's what I wanted. And I wanted it so badly that I couldn't comprehend the fact that that wasn't one of my choices. I finally had this epiphany that it was as if I were in a Chinese restaurant, pissed off because nobody would give me lasagna. I had two choices. I could stay, knowing it was abusive, and just not complain, even to myself. Or I could leave. But I could not stay there and expect it to be different."

Amy's husband had seen the letter on Monday. "By Thursday, the kids were gone and they weren't coming back. And he didn't know they weren't coming back, but they knew. Then I was gone on Saturday. And I couldn't drive because I shook all the time. A neighbor drove me and all of our pets down to Boise from where we lived in the mountains to our first little place. I rented a little house across the street from my mother's apartment building. It was five hundred dollars a month and truly should have been condemned, but it was so peaceful."

But while she was free from her husband's home, she was not free from her community's judgment.

"My husband was so charming in public. I remember once we were at the phase where I couldn't even really walk independently. I probably looked like the world's biggest bitch. As we're going to the car together, he's wanting to help me into the car. And I don't want him to touch me because I know that half a mile down the road, he's going to scream the whole hour-drive home. People that don't see all of it somehow seem to still think that they have the right to an opinion and to share it. And so that was one of the things for me: learning just to stop. I didn't have to explain. It didn't matter if they didn't believe me. It didn't matter if they didn't understand. I didn't have to justify my choices."

She was often shocked by the way listeners seemed to be worried—for her husband.

"If I had a nickel for every single person who said, *Well, do you think he has a mental illness? Have you tried to help him?* I spent seventeen years trying to help him. And by that point, I realized that the correlation between abuse and mental health was only something like seven percent. The average abusive man is not mentally ill. He's just mean. And my husband certainly has personality disorders, but there's nothing I can fix with chemicals. So he's not mentally ill, he's just mean."

She knew what people were really saying. "There's social pressure to stay," she says. "There's religious pressure to stay. There's the embarrassment factor because you didn't tell people, and so then you worry they won't believe. I used to wish he would hit me because then people would say I'd be justified to go."

A clear sign that Amy had made the right decision came just weeks after she'd moved her family to their new home.

"Three weeks after I left him, I could walk. I never had MS at all. What I had was actually technically called conversion disorder. If you live with enough stress and fear, your body will basically chew itself up. Sometimes people with that will have seizures. We used to call them pseudoseizures, and now they're called psychogenic, because pseudo sounds like, *We don't believe you, you're faking it.* The point is that conversion disorder is not faking. It's just what your body does to internalize fear, pain, and stress. The symptoms are real."

With her health improving, Amy was ready to abandon her stoicism and make changes.

"I went through a phase working on the Serenity Prayer, and I finally figured I had all the serenity I could stomach. I needed some strength and wisdom," she says.

A social worker told Amy about WISP. The prospect of going back to school seemed daunting at first, but Amy knew she had to make the leap. In the seventeen years she'd been in her abusive situation, the world had changed. Good jobs now called for a college degree.

"I had a high school diploma from 1985. And in 1985, I was able to get jobs with a high school diploma just because I was smart and worked hard and got along with people. It didn't take that much. When I left my husband, it took me six months to get a job in housekeeping. And there were three hundred applicants for two jobs because this was in 2008."

Even with a job, Amy struggled to get ahead. She started at $8.75 an hour. Then through hard work, she scored a promotion, moving up from housekeeping to registration, making $12 an hour. Amy was elated—until the other shoe dropped. Now, with a higher-paying job, she lost her eligibility for food stamps. Financially, she was back where she'd started.

Something had to change. Amy made the decision it would be a college degree. But it was no easy road.

"School was really hard. I went through school with three kids at home, and none of that was easy. Prior to even getting into nursing school, I was taking prereqs. I remember Walmart sent out a five-dollar gift card, like an advertising thing. I was in an apartment complex, hitting up all the trash cans and all the mail bins and picking those out of the trash," she says. "I remember how tight things were and how hard things were. I think WISP gave me about fifteen thousand dollars over the course of college. I still had school debt when I got out because I never made enough to actually support my kids while I was in school. But it got me to a place where I could take care of myself."

Amy completed her bachelor's in nursing and began working as a nurse. The support of WISP, the completion of her education, and her status as a professional allowed her to access the one thing she'd always wanted: freedom.

"Freedom, to me, boils down to the ability to make things happen the way I want," she says.

An education and a nursing job gave Amy the freedom to travel—something she now does routinely. "I discovered I actually love traveling. I just didn't like traveling with my ex-husband because anything that went wrong was my fault. The whole thing was no fun because I was either getting yelled at or trying to censor myself because I didn't want to get yelled at."

Her education also gave her the freedom to work at a job that gives her satisfaction and financial stability. She's happy her professional skills are in demand. She achieved the freedom to buy a big house for herself and she is able to take in family members as well. And she has the financial freedom to do what she likes and not be burdened by things she does not.

"It's lovely to be able to just make things happen that I want to have happen. If I need stuff that I would consider 'guy stuff,' I have guys I hire by the hour. I have a handyman. He shows up. He does what I ask him to do, I pay him, and he leaves. I have a guy that does 'car stuff.' I love what I do."

Amy has been able to help other women because she notices and names the invisible signs of abuse.

"I've helped two different women who weren't recognizing what they were seeing. I had a friend and we were out one evening, and I'm talking about something with my ex-husband. She said, *That's just like what my husband does.* And she told me more and more. I walked her through making a safety plan, having a bag packed by the door that he didn't know about." Having a plan and having a bag packed equals power, she says. "There's power if you can grab your bag and walk out the door. There is no power if you have to go into the bedroom and pack a bag. So when he threw a holy fit, she was able to say, *Don't use those words about me again or I'm going to have to leave.* And he said, *Is that a promise? Get out of my house, you effing bitch.*"

So she did. And rebuilt her life in another state.

In another situation, Amy helped a woman whose husband took away her access to cash, the car, and even her own identification. "I walked her through a safety plan so that she was able to get a replacement ID. And walked her through it all: *You have to not have that in the house. You have to hide these things.* It feels really good to be able to help somebody else understand that what they've got going on is not healthy and it's not going to change."

Amy has also been able to see the signs in her patients. "I have talked to a lot of patients and I routinely give out information about the domestic violence program in our area and information about WISP."

Amy never hesitates to pass on the wisdom she gained through experience. "I put down the secondhand shame I was carrying a long time ago. I'm proud to share my story. I'm very strong and I earned every bit of my strength and courage."

She remembers an activity she participated in at the domestic violence organization. "We would do T-shirts every fall. One year mine read, *Everybody always said he was such a nice guy.* Another featured an image of the ruby slippers from *The Wizard of Oz.* The quote read, *You've always had the power.*"

Like Dorothy, Amy realized she'd always had the power.

Freedom beyond Fear

Holly's Story

HOLLY HAS A UNIQUE relationship with fear.

"My therapist once said, *You are the weirdest anxiety person I've ever met.* Because I have an anxiety disorder, and I'll push through fear to confront it. And he said, *Most people shy away.*"

It's her inner courage that pushed her to escape her abuser, to pursue higher education, to break through personal barriers, and that informs the work she does today.

She's driven by a need to understand. "I want to know why. Why does this scare me? What do I not know? Because not knowing is the scariest thing to me. I need to see it. I need to touch it. I need to examine it. And then it's not so scary."

Confronting what is scariest was a core motivation for escaping her own abuse.

"I think that's what he took away from me—that drive. I lived in so much fear, and he knew that. He took so much power away from me and scared me so much. I was reclaiming a little bit more every time I pushed through that fear."

Holly is currently a PhD student in criminal justice with a 4.0 grade point average. But there was a time in her life when she was sure she was dumb and would never achieve academic excellence.

It was at one of the most challenging points in her life, living with her children in the basement of her parents' home after escaping her abusive husband, that she made a decision to try—in spite of what she believed about herself.

"I said, *They deserve a better life than I can give as a server and a single mom,*" she recalls. "I thought, *I don't care if I'm dumb. I'm going to get the help I need and I'm going to do this so that I can get a better job and do it for the kids.* My kids, absolutely, gave me the courage to do the things I truly believed I could not do."

Swallowing her fears and returning to college, she quickly learned she had underestimated her own abilities.

"I walked into the university apprehensive. I didn't think I could finish. I remember saying, *What tutoring services do you have? What extra support do you have? Because I don't think I'm smart enough to even finish this degree.*"

The representative replied that the institution was ready to offer plenty of support. But the first step was an assessment, to see where Holly should be placed.

What she learned surprised her.

"They came out with the results and I said, *Okay, give me the bad news.* And they said, *What bad news? You're a junior. You're exactly where you're supposed to be. You don't need any remedial services.*"

To her astonishment, she was ready to pick up where she'd left off in her college career.

Before she got started, though, she had more personal roadblocks to confront. Her next deterrent: affordability. She was on public assistance and though she was starting to think she might be smart enough to get her degree, paying for it seemed impossible. As she looked for scholarships online, she came across WISP. She worried WISP wouldn't want her as a recipient. Most of the scholarships she found were based on academic merit, and she told herself she didn't have what it takes. But the grim reality of her situation pushed her forward. "I thought, *I'm a single mom, two kids, one is literally an infant. I have to get this done!*"

She applied. She was approved. And that set the next act of her life in motion.

Staying true to form, rather than shy away from her experience as an abuse survivor, Holly let it guide her into the study of criminal justice. "I've always wanted to know, why do people do things? Why does one person who has a traumatic experience go into advocacy, but another becomes a criminal?"

Holly got her BA with the help of WISP. From there she went directly into a master's program.

"If you're going to be successful in criminal justice, you need more than a bachelor's; they're a dime a dozen. But a master's made you stand out. So I immediately applied for my master's—I think it was two weeks. I graduated and immediately started," Holly recalls. More than just the desire to beef up her resume, Holly knew she needed to keep her momentum if she was going to achieve her goals. "I knew that if I took any break I would probably not want to go back. It's hard to get started again. So I did my bachelor's and my master's, a single mom with two kids, working full time."

Her master's work continued to take her into new territory. "I was studying sex offenders, and I thought, *This scares me. Why does this bother me? What intrigues me about it?* And the obvious answer is, *Because you lived it. You're a survivor. So of course this is scary.* But I wanted to conquer that."

She also knew she wanted field experience, so she took a position in the substance abuse field. Later, a position in social work became available, and Holly decided to make the switch. It turned out to be a poor fit—although Holly found it illuminated important aspects of her own journey. "I was passionate and I loved it, but I also hated it because I saw myself way too much in the survivors. And I was nice to them outwardly, but inwardly very judgy to them because I saw too much of myself," she says. "I'm not saying I don't have empathy, and I'm not saying that my heart doesn't go out. But it was just too close. I couldn't distance myself."

That spurred Holly to seek out a new position—one that might seem surprising for an abuse survivor. But not if you know Holly. For her, the position made perfect sense. She could conquer her fear of working with offenders, and help survivors by making sure there are no more victims.

"I got a counselor position at the sex offender treatment prison here in Iowa. I knew: *I can do it. I can have my boundaries. I can empathize without being too nice.* It's actually very empowering to say, *You don't scare me anymore; you don't control me.* And then I help to hopefully change the future for people who have offended before and hopefully will never offend again."

She knew she was pursuing a path that not everyone would understand.

"I was so afraid to say that I worked with sex offenders because I never know how people are going to react to that," she says. "They're not the monsters that we think. They've done some terrible things. Absolutely. But the humanity is there. And ninety-nine-point-nine percent, I think, really want to change. They just don't know how. There is so little research on sex offenders and treatment and best practices. As I do my PhD, I find out that there's stuff six, seven years old, and you know how fast things change. I want to bring those monsters into the light and say, *What's true? What's not? And how do we make it better?*"

Society is often against that process. "We are so reactionary, and then we make the cycle worse because we give no chances. And I'm not saying that they should ever have a chance to reoffend. I don't ever want another victim, but I sometimes think we set them up to fail. If you don't give them housing or give them the ability to get housing, and you keep labeling them 'the monsters,' then what motivation do they have to change?"

Holly sees her work with sex offenders as the way she is able to be a force for good in her work and her community.

"I work with clients who have experienced tremendous trauma. I see in them potential. I see in them what WISP saw in me, someone who can do anything when given the opportunity and is willing to do the hard work." She recognizes the potential in some of the least redeemable members of society, giving sex offenders the chance to prove that they aren't what society says they are. A chance at redemption. A chance at life.

Holly is remarried now, to a man she says is "the love of my life, my best friend, my greatest cheerleader. I call my husband my safe place. That was monumental—that I would allow him to be my partner and allow him to see that I could be vulnerable and allow him to help me. I'm learning a new normal, and that is a blessing and scary.

"We decided to do everything all at once: get married, buy a house, attempt to get my PhD. And we were applying so that he could adopt my children. And I said, *You know what? This seems like an absolutely terrible time to try to get my PhD. But let's do it!*"

Once again, Holly faced her old fears of being unworthy as she made her way through the application process—seeking out programs, dealing with the challenging interview process, and getting some rejections. But she pushed through and secured an acceptance. And since starting her PhD program, she sees herself in a new light.

Her husband also challenges the way she feels about herself. "He holds a mirror up to me. He says, *You know, you're worth it.* And I say, *Oh, I hate it when you tell me that, and it's okay to feel these things.* And that is what he gives me. That's the healing part. Because I had to shut myself off a lot and focus on going forward. He makes me stop and really acknowledge my feelings."

She finally achieved her goal of making a final break from her abuser when, after a brutal battle for custody, he agreed to have his parental rights terminated. While the result is positive, she still thinks about what her abuser took from her, even in the final moments of the court proceedings.

"It was kind of hard because I wanted to tell my story. And I felt like this was one more thing that he took away. I wanted to testify. The adoption happened and healing started, for the kids and me. But I never got to testify. I never got to tell anybody my story other than to a therapist or my husband. I never got to put it out there. Now, I'm excited. I get to reclaim my story."

When Holly reflects on her journey to the present moment, she realizes an important shift has taken place. "At the time, I went back to school for my kids. I know that is not what you are supposed to say. You are supposed to say you did it for yourself. I wasn't there yet back then, but I'm not afraid to say it now. The courage I found to push through came from knowing that I had to do it for them to have a better life. And I continue to push through because fear and anxiety do not go away, but now I do it for myself.

"My husband says, *When you put your mind to it, I just step out of the way.* If I have an idea to do something and I've said it, it's just always going to happen. I don't do things small." Holly's message is one of courage and perseverance, whatever the motivation may be.

The Truth Will Set You Free

Tracey's Story

FOR TRACEY, the abuse is still hard to talk about.

"In the past, I wasn't allowed to share these stories. Speaking up or saying the wrong thing always resulted in some form of punishment," she explains. "Whenever the topic comes up, fear overwhelms me—fear of the repercussions. But I have to overcome that fear, every time."

And for a long time, Tracey existed in duality, torn between what she could acknowledge and what was really happening.

There was a disconnect between what she could talk about publicly and the reality of her home life. She struggled internally with being authentic versus inauthentic, and she had to do some serious mental gymnastics to stifle her truth. "I always saw myself as an authentic person, but I became someone who believed everything was great because I was told it was. I began to believe that it was my own perception that made me think something was wrong with what was happening."

This made every interaction a flirtation with danger. "It was like walking on a tightrope. Even if I was out to dinner with a friend, saying something incorrectly had the potential to get back to my abuser, which could have resulted in consequences. I know this is a common experience among abuse survivors," she says. "My abuser was that classic charismatic person, always the fun one at the party, very respected in our society, our community. When I reached out to mutual acquaintances for help, I often got turned away. In private, people would say, *Oh, this is just a problem between you and him. Oh, he's a nice guy. Yeah, divorce is hard.*

"Over the years, I've tried to find compassion for those people too. I had lied to them, never revealing what was really happening at home, acting like we were just great, that everything was just great. So when I finally shared my true story, it blindsided them." This duality served as a protective measure. Until she separated herself from her abuser, it wasn't safe for Tracey to speak her truth.

The power and control dynamic that is characteristic of every abusive relationship often starts gradually, often imperceptibly. This was Tracey's experience. "When I first met my abuser, he told me how he was going to help me reach my goals, and in return, I gave him everything that he asked for. Over time, however, the inconsistencies between his promises and actions grew bigger, and my ability to question them grew less. My ideas, if he liked them, would become his rather than my own. My right to make my own decisions, behave in ways that he did not approve of, or follow my own dreams slowly disappeared. Any objections that I had would be met with consequences. Eventually, I learned that it was safer to be quiet and give up my own goals, including my career, and sacrifice my self-worth."

When she finally did work up the courage to seek help, the counselor had to first break through the psychological barriers Tracey had built.

"I called an organization in our town, even though I was fully convinced that I was wrong to make the appointment. I talked to the intake counselor for several hours. I said that I was just crazy and not in an abusive relationship. Luckily, that intake counselor didn't listen to me and set me up with a therapist."

But even with that breakthrough, Tracey found she had to take progress one small step at a time. Even when she'd made the decision to go back to school and was offered the opportunity to apply for a WISP scholarship, the old ghost came back to haunt her. She had to face the thing that remained most difficult for her—talking about the abuse.

The ingrained habit of staying silent was so powerful that even financial pressure couldn't budge it.

"I was struggling financially at the time, yet I still couldn't bring myself to fill out the application. I started going back to school, and I think I held on to that application for almost a year before I turned it in."

Some of the questions in the application left her stumped. But they also forced her out of her frozen, speechless state.

"The thing I kept getting stuck on was the question about describing the abuse. That question was so hard because I had learned to hide it away. In hindsight, I'm kind of grateful for that difficult question," she says. "I also remember one of the requirements was that you had to have left the relationship. That was a tough one for me because I had been out of the relationship quite a while, but I was experiencing postseparation abuse. Back then, I didn't know those words, but I do now."

In the end, Tracey overcame her fear of telling the truth and submitted her application. The scholarship from WISP was more than just financial aid. It was validation that her story was true and that she was worthy of support. "This wasn't my first degree. I had an entire career before I ever met my abuser. The first time I went to school at a younger age, I received a number of academic scholarships, and I was taught back then that a scholarship was something you deserved and it was given to you because you earned it. It was given to you in a positive light, signifying that you are somehow worthy of getting that scholarship," she says. "With WISP, the monetary part helped a lot. But it was more of the psychological and emotional benefit for me." Tracey had duped herself into thinking what she perceived and experienced in her relationship wasn't real—that she was wrong. The validation she received from WISP challenged the story she'd had to adopt in order to stay safe in the abusive relationship. She began to merge the duality she'd lived in for so long.

Tracey chose to pursue a master's degree in nonprofit leadership and management. This degree path would turn out to be of help to her in surprising ways.

She found out that leadership is all about relationships. "Being part of a group of people studying leadership, I realized most of the foundation of our program was focusing on relationships. We were looking at it from a nonprofit view, and talking about our relationships with donors, clients, and staff, and explored what kind of leader we wanted to be and how you achieve that." This information was highly relevant to dealing with the repercussions of disentangling herself from a narcissistic partner.

School was another voice that countered the negative messages she had come to believe were true. It was another crack in her story, that duality that she had constructed. "I had so much invested in getting this degree. I felt I had to succeed because I had this person waiting for me to fail," she says. "I poured a lot into my studies and I ended up doing really well because it wasn't just the next notch in my career ladder. It wasn't just something that my job required me to do. It was a life commitment for me. I received a lot of positive feedback from the people I worked with. And in the beginning—I say in the beginning, but I'm probably lying, it was probably all the way through—it was really hard for me to hear that because it was so against what I had come to believe."

Even as Tracey was making strides toward healing and establishing her life free from abuse, her abuser sought to keep his negative hold on her.

"I was being taken to court constantly—every two to three months. He switched his power to the courtroom. I was trapped because we had a child together, and I was stuck in this world. I was in court hearings about how worthless I was, how I had mental health issues, and how I was incapable of parenting; the list goes on and on. Family court was believing a lot of this. My desire to go back to school was used in a very negative way. I was told I was trying to be a career student who was trying to avoid supporting our child."

His constant criticism influenced the court proceedings. The judge bought the story that she was using school as a means to avoid parental responsibilities so he made her see an outside evaluator—who ended up being an ally. It was another hurdle Tracey needed to clear before she could do what she knew was best.

And she did. Finally, with court approval, Tracey went to graduate school while juggling the responsibilities of a single mother. She had to come up with creative strategies to fit in with many of her classmates.

"I remember working on group projects in our cohort. I would always say to people, *I can't meet you at seven p.m. for the group project, but I will have this in an email to you by six a.m.* I did most of my studies at two in the morning, and it became a part of the routine. It was not possible for me to do it otherwise," she says.

At first, she still found herself living the duality—having one life she showed to her classmates and another she kept private. But over the course of her studies, she began to merge her two realities and show the world her true experience. "These were people that didn't know me in my previous life. They knew that I had a child because my kiddo might come to class. They knew that part, but they didn't know all the stuff going on behind the scenes," she says. "I started integrating my own story into my degree. I really feel like the scholarship helped me do that, because it stayed in the back of my mind: *I can share something about domestic violence. Because I know a little bit about it.*" Again, the support she received from WISP became a form of validation. People she'd never met before could acknowledge her experience and her hard-earned wisdom. "It was like giving me permission, in a way."

She took the effort one step further when she decided to write her final paper on the topic of family court—drawing inspiration from her own experience and her vision of what that system could be.

"I ended up writing about the leadership that I saw in the family court," she says. The disparity between what she'd experienced and who she was in her classes became part of that story. "It was definitely integrated. It's how my story started to become apparent to the people I was working with. Because we might have a project due in two days, but I would get called into an emergency hearing, and since I was representing myself I'd say, *We might have to put things on hold for a couple of days.* These kinds of things happened constantly throughout my entire degree. I ended up bringing those two pieces together, talking about ideas for a utopian court experience, where transactional leadership becomes transformational leadership in the courtroom."

Tracey graduated in 2020. Now, having completed college and graduate school, she continues working to overcome her fears and share her story. She has spoken at city council meetings to raise awareness around domestic violence and finds that each time she speaks, the words come more freely. Today she has the ability to say, "This conversation or story might get out there. But as long as I present it in such a way that I can be proud of it, it doesn't matter what somebody else might try to do with it in a negative way."

Tracey took ownership of her own story. She controls the narrative now. Her example carries this message: Speak with your singular, authentic voice.

Thank You

FOCUSING ON GRATITUDE HAS a slew of well-documented benefits, but for Doris, saying thank you was more about manners than mindset. She was a staunch advocate for the rules of etiquette and firmly believed that a gift ought to be acknowledged. It's polite, and in certain circles, it's expected. When an applicant accepts her scholarship award, she is required to write a thank-you note to Doris Buffett. This was Doris's way of teaching recipients how to meet those expectations, preparing them for jobs and a future after the isolation and control of abuse.

Every few weeks we would mail Doris a bulging envelope stuffed full of the cards and notes we'd collected. And she'd read them all. It wasn't unusual to receive a call from Doris with a question or a comment about something she read, and when that happened, we had better have an answer—the right one, and fast. She had a deep, personal interest in each of the women who were part of WISP.

Although she is no longer here to read those notes, we continue to require them. It's part of Doris's legacy.

They are moving testimony to the power of one action. One gift that keeps on giving.

Without your generosity and hard work, I would not have been able to change the lives of my son and myself. Everyone I have worked with through WISP has been kind, helpful, understanding, and motivating. I am more than happy to be another success story from the WISP program, and I am honored for the opportunity to be able to be selected for such a life-changing scholarship. I went from working at slightly above minimum wage to having a career and stability. Having an education has not only improved my life, but it opens up the door to creating the best life possible for my child, which he deserves so much.

—Alexandra

I would like to say thank you for helping me achieve my goals. I once had a dream about finishing my college degree, and with help from WISP, I no longer have a dream, I have a goal. A goal that is realistic in attaining and that soon will become a reality. I can't wait for my children to see how I overcame the obstacles life threw our way and help so many others that are where I have been. Thank you for believing in me and helping me be able to achieve getting my degree. After losing everything, I tell my children that your education is something that no one can take away from you. The WISP scholarship has given me a second chance, given my kids a second chance. With more gratitude than I could ever express in words, thank you!

—Amber

It has been such a pleasure to be in school for the past two-and-a-half years. I have met many outstanding professors and peers. I am beyond grateful to have been able to be awarded this scholarship as I will graduate with zero student debt. That has been such a weight off of my shoulders while trying to raise a teenager and be a single parent. I look forward to this next chapter in my life. I continue daily to thank God for all the blessings and people that have been involved in this journey with me! I could not have done this without the help of WISP and all the wonderful women who have helped along the way!

—Kayla

This last semester has been difficult as I have struggled with health-related problems and expenses. WISP has never let me down and continues to help as they have granted me emergency funds and given me necessary help as I finish my MSW. I have never been more grateful to an organization.

In school, I learned about the Holmes-Rahe scale and how certain kinds of stress can lead to health issues. With the challenges I had with my abusive ex-husband, I believe this has contributed to these problems. However, because WISP cares about each individual in their organization, I know I can overcome my past and have it lead to a healthy and bright future.

Thank you, WISP, for helping me lead a life of blue skies.

—Tessa

I would like to extend my gratitude to the WISP scholarship for their unwavering support throughout my academic tenure. It is with great admiration that I reflect on Ms. Doris Buffett at this time; her dedication to philanthropy has allowed me to achieve my educational goals thus far. I am thankful for the compassionate and supportive staff at WISP. The legacy Ms. Doris Buffett has planted and nurtured over the course of her lifespan has blossomed into a force that continues to propel women like me toward financial freedom. I am grateful for the social opportunities that were made possible through higher education supported by the WISP scholarship.

—Anonymous

Thank you for believing and supporting me to pursue my dreams. Your benevolence is a gift that will be remembered for generations to come. There is a saying that says, *Everyone has a story.* You are forever part of my story; whenever it is my turn to tell my story, WISP is included. Nobody gets anywhere without help, and we are all one. You are not just part of my journey; you are part of my family and me.

—Adelaide

Epilogue

DORIS BUFFETT, even with her privilege, wasn't immune to difficulties in her life. Yet she found a way to channel her pain into work that has had a profound impact on the world around her. The reverberations of her gift—the gift of WISP—are still being felt today.

All of the women in this book were influenced by that gift. Receiving a scholarship from WISP was a catalyst for change in their lives. Their stories demonstrate that others, too, found ways to channel their hardships into something worthwhile, something beneficial, something that positively impacts others, in immeasurable ways, infinitely. Their stories are evidence that beauty can be found in painful places. And maybe more importantly—that beauty is not in spite of the pain, it's because of it.

What seems to be broken is what makes each of us beautiful.

This is your invitation to see things differently. Can you find the beauty in the pain? Will you allow those seemingly broken parts to show you the way to your gifts, the ones that belong only to you, that only you can share with others? These are the gifts that will create infinite ripples of goodwill that will touch others in countless ways, with amazing results.

If you follow the lead of the women in this book, you'll know that transformation is within reach.

You'll know it isn't a simple process. You'll know that the road to transformation is long, winding, full of pitfalls—and so very worth it.

Let their stories serve as a catalyst—if they can do it, so can you.

Heartbreak is the price of being human. How you piece your heart back together is entirely up to you.

Acknowledgments

IF LOVE WERE A CURRENCY, I'd be one of the wealthiest people in the world. My life is rich in relationships, and in my opinion, that's far more valuable than dollars. There's not enough space to list everyone who has blessed me with their presence, but if you read this, I think you'll know who you are. Know, too, that I will forever be grateful for you. Mom, your interest in the stories and your eagerness to read them was the encouragement I needed to get started and keep going. Chris, leader of my PR team and president of my fan club, your enthusiasm for this project—and anything I do, honestly—is a gift straight from the heart. Russ, this project took a lot of my time and attention, and you handled the changes without complaint. Thank you for offering extra help when I needed it. I'm the luckiest mom. Joe Z. and my heart-to-heart family, you are a weekly reminder that beauty grows from the seeds of despair. Thank you for helping me become visible. Ash, my soul-sister, thank you for lending your brilliant professional expertise and your gentle, loving support to this project.

So many people rallied to my cause, which was a truly humbling and heartening experience. Susan, you forged the path and I followed. Thank you for being a compass, pointing me in the right direction. Ellen, you are the taskmaster I needed to move this project along. Thank you for being the boss of me. You dove deep into these stories with me and tossed me a lifeline when I felt like I was drowning. Jennifer, your encyclopedic knowledge of all things grammar is astounding. Your expertise made this a better book. Laura D., Laura C., and Leslie, you three jumped when I asked you to and came through with beautiful results. Tammy, Amy, and Livia, you have been hearing about this book for many, many months and never failed to be interested, enthusiastic, and supportive. I thank my lucky stars that I'm part of our small but mighty team.

To the women who shared their stories with me, this book would not exist without you. Your generosity knows no bounds and is only exceeded by your courage. It has been a joy and an honor to collaborate with you. To the artists and writers who contributed their talents to this project, you put your hearts and souls into what you create. Eugenia, Rebecca, and Stephanie, thank you for sharing your gifts with me and with the world. To every WISP recipient I've crossed paths with for the last twenty-plus years, you have given me just as much as you have received as a scholar and maybe more. There's no way I can adequately express my thanks and admiration.

Last but certainly not least, to Doris Buffett, the Queen Bee herself, I hope that you are watching us from "The Great Beyond" and approve of our continued efforts to uphold your legacy. When you created WISP, you brought together an extraordinary group of women and granted us the privilege of doing work that changes lives. Little did I know how my own life would change when I answered that ad in the classified section of the Sunday paper back in 2003. Thank you for the opportunity—it's been an amazing adventure.

Jill Tremlett Large

SINCE JOINING THE WOMEN'S INDEPENDENCE SCHOLARSHIP PROGRAM in 2003, Jill Tremlett Large has been inspired by working with women who are achieving success despite seemingly insurmountable challenges. Jill was presented with her own opportunity to overcome impossible circumstances when, in 2009, she became a mother and a widow in the space of ten days. In the depth of the grief and turmoil that followed, she made a vow to live life to the fullest, and in the process of doing so, she discovered that by facing our deepest pain we equally increase our capacity for joy. Always one for a good story, she has often been asked if she is writing a book. Finally, the answer to that question is *yes*.

Women's Independence Scholarship Program

THE WOMEN'S INDEPENDENCE SCHOLARSHIP PROGRAM is the brainchild of the late Doris Buffett and, for twenty-five years, has provided scholarships to survivors of intimate partner abuse solely through the benefit of her generosity and foresight. Doris was a no-nonsense, practical, and pragmatic Midwesterner who staunchly believed in leveling the playing field and leveraged her personal fortune to do so. Since 1999, her gift of WISP has touched the lives of thousands of individuals, families, and communities, rippling forward in countless ways and leaving a legacy of caring for others.